THE ESSENTIAL GUIDE
TO CATHOLIC TERMS

THE ESSENTIAL GUIDE
TO CATHOLIC TERMS

Mary Kathleen Glavich, SND

LOYOLAPRESS.
A JESUIT MINISTRY

Chicago

LOYOLA PRESS.
A JESUIT MINISTRY

3441 N. Ashland Avenue
Chicago, Illinois 60657
(800) 621-1008
www.loyolapress.com

Cover art credit: Rafael Lopez.

ISBN-13: 978-0-8294-4064-5
ISBN-10: 0-8294-4064-X
Library of Congress Control Number: 2013954728

Printed in the United States of America.

13 14 15 16 17 18 Versa 10 9 8 7 6 5 4 3 2 1

Introduction

Mathematicians, sailors, crocheters, athletes, cooks, police offi-
cers—every group has its jargon, or own way of discussing their way of
life. Catholics, too, have our own vocabulary. For children still learning and mastering English, Catholic terms can be mystifying. *Is an
epistle the wife of an apostle? How can birds elect a pope?*

For some adults, it has been many years since they learned certain
terms and could use a refresher. Some adults harbor misperceptions
about the Immaculate Conception and confuse the Ascension with the
Assumption. To further complicate matters, some common English
words, like *grace*, have different meanings in the context of our faith.
Furthermore, some Catholic terms derive from other languages, such
as Latin (*ex cathedra*), Hebrew (*hosanna*), and Greek (*paraclete*).

The Essential Guide to Catholic Terms offers complete, clear expla-
nations of Catholic words from *abbot* to *zucchetto*. Children, parents,
teachers, directors of religious education, and librarians will find this
book to be a handy reference when they encounter an unfamiliar word
in a homily, a homework assignment, or Catholic reading material. Or
try reading the book from the beginning to discover new terms and
concepts you didn't already know! You may just find that learning the
meaning of more Catholic words leads to a deeper understanding and
love of Jesus, the ultimate Word!

Using This Book

Some entries contain terms in **boldface** print.
You can find out more about a topic by looking
up these words too.

Glossary

A

abbey

The monastery where **monks**[*] live and the convent where **nuns** live is called an abbey.

abbot/abbess

An abbot is the man who is the elected head of a community of **monks**. The word *abbot* comes from *abba*, which means "father." The woman who is the head of a community of **nuns** is an abbess.

Abraham

Did you know that Jews, Christians, and Muslims are related? Each religion claims Abraham as its great father, or **patriarch**. He lived in the Middle East about two thousand years before Jesus. God entered into an agreement (or **covenant**) with Abraham and promised him as many descendants as there are stars and grains of sand. He would be the father of many nations and kings; all nations would be blessed by his offspring. God also told Abraham that the land of Canaan would be his.

Abraham showed great faith. When Abraham and his wife Sarah were very, very old, they had a son named Isaac. When God tested Abraham by telling him to sacrifice Isaac, Abraham prepared to do so, but God didn't let him go through with it. Because Abraham worshipped the one, true God, he is the root of your family tree of faith. Isaac had two sons, Jacob and Esau. Jacob had twelve sons, whose families became the twelve tribes of Israel. From Jacob's son Judah came the tribe that included King **David**, whose descendants include **Joseph**

---

[*] You can find out more about a topic by looking up the words in boldface.

and Jesus. The prophet Mohammed is a descendant of Abraham's son Ishmael, whose mother was Hagar, Sarah's maid.

See Genesis chapters 15 and 22 for the story of Abraham.

absolution

We feel better when the person we hurt says, "I forgive you." Absolution is God's forgiveness of sin. The Gospels show that Jesus forgave people's sins. After his Resurrection, Jesus appeared to the Apostles and gave them—and through them, all priests—the power and authority to offer absolution. In the Sacrament of **Penance**, we hear the priest say the words of absolution in the name of Jesus. Then our guilt and shame are taken away for good.

See Mark 2:1–12 about Jesus absolving a man of sin.

abstinence

Abstinence is the religious practice of not consuming certain food or drink. Not allowing ourselves to have something we like is a way to show that we want to make up for sin. It also builds self-control. During **Lent**, Catholics who are older than fourteen abstain from meat on Fridays and on Ash Wednesday. For many years Catholics abstained from meat every Friday as **penance** in memory of the Lord's suffering and death. Today we are no longer required to abstain from meat, but we must still perform some kind of penance.

Acts of the Apostles

The Acts of the Apostles is a book of the **Bible** that is just what the title says—a record of the **Apostles'** actions. Scripture scholars think that the author of Acts also wrote the Gospel of Luke. Acts tells the story of the early Church from the time of the **Ascension** of Jesus. Another title for this book could be the Book of the **Holy Spirit** because it describes the coming of the Holy Spirit at **Pentecost** and shows the Spirit's key role in the Church as the Apostles preached, spread the

Gospel to other lands, and accepted Gentiles as members. Most of Acts recounts St. **Paul's** conversion and his missionary journeys.

actual grace

See **grace**.

Adam

We meet Adam in Genesis, the first book of the Bible. Adam is the first human being. His name comes from the Hebrew word for "earth" because God created Adam from earth. Then God made Eve as a companion to Adam from one of Adam's own ribs. God made Adam and Eve in his likeness and image. That means that they had a mind to think and a will to love. This first couple was created holy. God's plan was that people would know him and love him and live with him forever. God put all other creatures on earth into their care. Sadly, Adam and Eve disobeyed God. They ate the fruit that God had forbidden them to eat. Consequently our first parents lost God's friendship and could no longer live with him in **Paradise**. They lost their special gifts and became weak against **temptation**. They also had to work hard, suffer, and someday die. This first sin of Adam affected all his children, including you. That is why we needed a Savior. Jesus is called the new or second Adam.

See Genesis 2:7—3:24 for the story of Adam.

adoration

Adoration is the worship we give to **God** alone because he is the supreme and perfect being. We also owe God adoration because he is our Creator and Savior. The First Commandment tells us to adore God alone. We express adoration by words of praise and by actions, such as genuflecting before the tabernacle. Do you see why it doesn't make sense to say things like "I adore your outfit"?

Advent

Advent is the first season of the **liturgical year** and lasts about four weeks. It is the time when we prepare to celebrate Christmas. The word *Advent* means "coming." During Advent we think and pray about the three comings of Christ: in history at Bethlehem; in mystery every day, especially in the Eucharist; and in majesty at the end of the world. We might make an **Advent wreath** and pray the **O Antiphons**. During the weeks before Christmas, many people concentrate on Santa Claus and gifts. A good Advent helps us focus on Jesus, the greatest gift.

Advent wreath

During Advent you might see an Advent wreath in church. Its circular shape symbolizes God, who has no beginning or end. It is a wreath of evergreen, which doesn't "die" in winter but stays green, the color of life. The evergreen also reminds us that God is eternal. Four candles are set in the wreath. Usually three candles are purple, the color for Advent, and one is pink for the third week that begins with Gaudete (Rejoice) Sunday. A white bow may be placed at the foot of each candle. Each week of Advent, we light a new candle and pray a prayer asking Jesus to come. During the fourth week, all four candles are burning. Sometimes a large white candle is placed in the center of the wreath as a Christ candle that is lit on Christmas Eve.

alb

An alb is a long white robe that leaders wear at the **liturgy**. It is worn under other special garments and is usually tied at the waist with a cincture, or rope. The word *alb* comes from the Latin word for "white." If you are an altar server, you might wear an alb. At the Easter Vigil, newly baptized Christians also may be clothed in an alb as a sign of their new life in Christ.

All Saints Day

Imagine the billions of people who are in **Heaven**. Only a few of these saints are **canonized** and have their own feast day. The Church made November 1 a feast to celebrate all the saints, including your relatives who are with God. The word *hallowed* means "holy." Hallowed ones are the saints. Halloween began as All Hallows Eve, the day before All Saints Day, just as Christmas Eve is the day before Christmas. All Saints Day is a **Holy Day of Obligation** in the United States unless it falls on a Saturday or a Monday.

All Souls Day

On All Souls Day, November 2, we remember all the faithful who have died. We pray that the people who are in **Purgatory** may soon enjoy eternal life with God. On All Souls Day, Catholics go to Mass and visit cemeteries. In Mexico and some other countries, it is the Day of the Dead, celebrated with parades, shrines, costumes, and food.

Alleluia

Alleluia is a word of joy that means "Praise the Lord." In Hebrew, the word *hallel* means "praise," and *Yah* is the first syllable of Yahweh, thought to be God's personal name. We sing Alleluia at Mass before the Gospel is proclaimed. During **Lent** we do not speak this happy word, but then at Easter we say and sing it over and over to rejoice in the Resurrection of Jesus. Saint Augustine said that a Christian should be an alleluia from head to toe.

almsgiving

You've probably heard the expression "alms for the poor." Almsgiving is the act of donating money or goods to those who are needy. It shows love for God and others. **Prayer**, **fasting**, and almsgiving are the three chief Lenten practices.

Alpha and Omega

The Alpha (A) and Omega (Ω) are the first and last letters of the Greek alphabet, like our A and Z. In the Bible they are names for God and Jesus. The Alpha reflects that nothing existed before God, and the Omega means that God is our final end. God is the beginning and the end of all. At the Easter Vigil the priest carves an Alpha and Omega into the **Paschal Candle**. He prays, "Christ yesterday and today, the beginning and the end, Alpha and Omega, all time belongs to him and all the ages. To him be glory and power through every age for ever. Amen."

See Revelation 1:8 and 22:13 to read more about God as Alpha and Omega.

altar

An altar is a table on which a **sacrifice** is offered to God. The altar used for the sacrifice of Jesus at Mass is the most important structure in the church. It is also the table on which Jesus gives himself to us as food. A white linen cloth covers the altar. Some altars have **relics** of saints set inside or under them. At the beginning and end of Mass the priest kisses the altar. We bow whenever we pass before it. This is because the altar is holy and stands for Christ. When a new altar is consecrated, it is anointed with **Chrism**, a holy oil. A May altar is a small shrine constructed to honor Mary. It is not a true altar because sacrifices are not offered on it.

ambo

The lectern or pulpit in church is also called an ambo. It is the stand near the altar from which the Scripture and Gospel readings are read, where the Homily is given, and where the Universal Prayer (Prayer of the Faithful) is prayed.

ambry

An ambry is a special cabinet for the three **holy oils: Chrism**, the oil of the catechumens, and the oil of the sick. It is usually in the **sanctuary** of a church.

Amen

We say Amen after a prayer. You might think it means "the end." Actually *Amen* is a Hebrew word that means "certainly" or "I believe." Jesus sometimes said Amen twice before speaking. This let people know that what he was about to say was very important. At Mass, at the end of the Eucharistic Prayer, we wholeheartedly say or sing the Great Amen. We also say Amen as an act of faith in the presence of Jesus when we receive Holy Communion.

angel

An angel is a majestic, powerful, and wise being created by God. Like God, an angel is a pure **spirit** who is invisible but who can take on a body to appear to us. Artists draw wings on angels to show that they can move quickly. Angels are in the presence of God in **Heaven**, constantly praising him and serving him. There are a vast number of them. According to tradition, angels are ranked in nine choirs, or groups. The two highest, or closest to God, are seraphim and cherubim. Then there are the thrones, dominions, virtues, powers, principalities, archangels, and angels.

The word *angel* means "messenger." In the Bible, God sends angels to act as his agents. Three **archangels**, or chief angels, appear in the Bible and are named: Saint Michael, Saint **Gabriel**, and Saint Raphael. God assigns each person a **guardian angel** to watch over and pray for him or her. Angels who rebelled against God and so are forever separated from him are called **devils**.

See Matthew 1:18–23 and 2:13–22 to read how an angel guided Saint Joseph.

Angelus

The Angelus is a prayer that celebrates the **Incarnation**. It takes its name from the first sentence, "The angel of the Lord declared unto Mary." Formerly the Angelus was prayed at 6:00 a.m., noon, and 6:00 p.m., and some religious communities continue this practice. During the prayer, bells ring nine times in sets of three. It's long been a custom to ring church bells to remind people to pray the Angelus.

Annunciation

The Annunciation of the Lord is the mystery of the angel Gabriel announcing the **Incarnation** to Mary. He reveals that she will have a baby. Her child will have no earthly father but will be the Son of God through the power of the Holy Spirit. She is to name him Jesus, and he will be the **Messiah** and our Savior. Mary accepts God's will, calling herself his handmaid, or servant. We celebrate the Annunciation on March 25. In Nazareth, in Israel, a large church stands on the site where tradition holds that the Word (God) was made flesh (man).

See Luke 1:26–38 for the story of the Annunciation.

anointing

When you were baptized, you were anointed. Anointing is the religious ceremony of pouring or rubbing oil on people and things to mark them for a sacred purpose. The Hebrews anointed priests, prophets, and kings. An anointing takes place in the sacraments of Baptism, Confirmation, Holy Orders, and the Anointing of the Sick. Jesus is called the Christ, which means "the anointed one." In the synagogue of Nazareth, Jesus stated that he was anointed by the Spirit of the Lord.

See Luke 4:18–21 for the story of Jesus proclaiming his anointing.

Anointing of the Sick

Jesus healed all kinds of sick people. Today he still helps those who are ill or injured through the Sacrament of the Anointing of the Sick.

People who are very old or in poor health or who face serious surgery can be anointed by a priest. The priest traces the **Sign of the Cross** with the oil of the sick on their forehead and palms. This sacrament comforts the person, prepares him or her for death, and sometimes brings about a physical healing. When possible, confessing sins and receiving Holy Communion are included in the sacrament. If the Holy Communion is the person's last one, it is called **viaticum**. Anointing can be celebrated at home, in a hospital, or in church. We show support and love when someone is anointed by being present and praying.

See James 5:13–16 for the early Church's practice of this sacrament.

Antichrist

The Antichrist is the enemy of Christ who will appear before the second coming. He will draw people away from God. Scripture refers a few times to the Antichrist, but who he is remains a mystery. Various historical figures have been identified as the Antichrist because they were so hateful and deliberately opposed to the message of Jesus.

antiphon (AN-ti-fahn)

An antiphon is a short prayer, usually a Scripture verse, which is said or sung before and after a **psalm** or **canticle** or between its verses. It is related to the theme of the psalm or canticle.

Apocalypse

See **Revelation**.

apocryphal books

The Church set the canon, or official list, of books in the Bible at the Council of Trent in 1546. Early Christian books that were not accepted as divinely inspired are called apocryphal. These include the Gospel of Thomas, the Protoevangelium of James, the Shepherd of Hermas, and the Epistle of Barnabas.

apologist

An apologist is someone who explains and defends the teachings of the Church. He or she strives to show that its **doctrines** are reasonable. Saint Augustine of Hippo and Saint Thomas Aquinas are two outstanding apologists.

apostasy

Apostasy is the complete rejection of the Christian faith by one who was a believer. The person who gives up the faith is called an apostate.

Apostle

Did you know that Jesus was an apostle? An apostle is one who is sent out on a **mission**. Jesus is an apostle because he was sent to earth by the Father. Ordinarily, though, the word *Apostle* means one of the twelve men Jesus chose and taught to witness to him and his Resurrection and to carry on his work. The Apostles are **Peter**, Andrew, James, John, Matthew, Simon, Jude, Thomas, James the Less, Philip, Bartholomew, and Matthias, who replaced Judas. St. **Paul** is called the Apostle to the Gentiles. The Apostles spread the Good News about Jesus and were leaders in the early Church. All the Apostles except John were martyred, that is, killed for the faith. Our **bishops** are the successors to the Apostles.

See Matthew 27:16–20 for the story of Jesus commissioning his Apostles.

Apostles' Creed

See **creed**.

apse

An apse is the area at the end of a church where the altar is located and the **clergy** are seated. Often the walls of an apse form a semicircle, and the ceiling is domed. Apses like these are mostly found in the large churches in Europe and in **cathedrals** and **basilicas**.

archangel

An archangel is one of the seven chief angels. From Scripture we know of Saints Michael, Gabriel, and Raphael. Michael, whose name means "who is like God," led the good angels in the war against the devil and protects the Church today. Gabriel, whose name means "strength of God," was sent by God to announce to Mary that she was chosen to be the Mother of Jesus, the Savior. Raphael, whose name means "God heals," accompanied Tobias on a journey and healed his wife and father. September 29 is the Feast of Saints Michael, Gabriel, and Raphael.

See the Book of Tobit to read a story about the archangel Raphael.

ark

1) The ark is a huge boat that God instructed Noah to build as a means to save him and his family during the Flood. It is a symbol of the Church, through which God saves us by the waters of **Baptism**.

2) The Ark of the Covenant was a gold-covered chest that God told **Moses** to build. On top of the Ark, two gold cherubim (**angels**) with outspread wings faced each other. God was present for the Israelites at the Ark in the same way that he is present for us in our **tabernacles**. The Ark held the tablets of the Ten **Commandments** and was carried by the Israelites on their desert journey. King **David** had the Ark brought to Jerusalem. When King Solomon built the Temple in Jerusalem, the Ark was placed inside. This Temple was destroyed by enemies, and the Ark of the Covenant disappeared.

Ascension

Ascend means "to go up." The Ascension is the mystery of Jesus' return to Heaven forty days after the Resurrection. The **Acts of the Apostles** tells how the Apostles saw Jesus lifted up in his humanity. Now he is seated at the right hand of the Father in glory forever. We celebrate Ascension Thursday forty days after Easter. It is a **Holy Day of Obligation**.

See Acts of the Apostles 1:6–11 for the story of the Ascension.

Ash Wednesday

Ashes have been a symbol of **repentance** since Old Testament times. Ash Wednesday is the first day of Lent, a season of repentance before Easter. It is not a **Holy Day of Obligation**, but we must **fast** and **abstain** from meat. Many Catholics do go to church on this day to receive ashes. The priest blesses the ashes, and then he or someone else traces the Sign of the Cross with them on each person's forehead. As the cross is made, one of two things is said: "Turn away from sin and be faithful to the Gospel" or "Remember that thou art dust, and to dust thou shalt return." The ashes come from burning the blessed palms from the previous year's **Passion (Palm) Sunday**. They are a **sacramental**.

Assumption

The Assumption is the Catholic **dogma** that after Mary's life on earth was finished, she went to Heaven body and soul. When we die, we will not be united with our bodies until the end of the world. The Assumption is one of the privileges that Mary enjoyed because she is the Mother of God. We celebrate the Assumption on August 15.

B

banns

Banns are the public announcements in church of a couple's intent to marry. They occur on the three Sundays before the wedding. The practice began as a way to discover if there was any reason why the two people should not be wed. As of 1983, banns are no longer required, but you might still see them printed in church bulletins.

Baptism

You probably don't remember your Baptism because most people are baptized as infants. Baptism is a Sacrament of Initiation into the Church and the first and most necessary sacrament. It unites us with Jesus and through his Death and Resurrection makes us children of God and heirs of **Heaven**. It also makes us Christians, members of the **Church** founded by Jesus Christ. Through Baptism **Original Sin** is wiped away along with any other sin, and we are filled with **grace**, which is God's life. The Trinity lives within us. We also receive the **virtues** of faith, hope, and love and the **Gifts of the Holy Spirit**. Baptism leaves a permanent spiritual mark in us called a baptismal **character**. We may be baptized only once. Baptized people are entitled to celebrate the other **sacraments**.

The word *baptism* means "washing." In the rite of Baptism, a priest pours water over the head of the person three times and says, "I baptize you in the name of the Father, and of the Son, and of the Holy Spirit." Sometimes a person is immersed in a pool instead. In an emergency, anyone can perform a Baptism. At Baptism we receive our name, and we (or our godparents on our behalf) **vow** that we reject sin and believe in the faith of the Church. We receive a candle lit from the **Paschal (Easter) Candle** to represent the light of faith that we are now to pass on. We also wear a white garment, a symbol of our new life in Christ.

When it is impossible to receive Baptism with water, there are two other forms. Baptism of blood occurs when a non-baptized person is martyred because of his or her belief in Christ. Baptism of desire occurs when a person intends to accept the faith but dies before being baptized with water.

See Mark 1:9–11 for the story of Jesus' baptism, which shows that he was ready to stand with us sinners as our Savior.

basilica

A basilica is a large, important church. Rome has the four major (or highest-ranking) basilicas: St. Peter's, St. John Lateran, St. Mary Major, and St. Paul Outside the Walls. These have holy doors that are only opened during **Jubilee** Years. Many other basilicas attract pilgrims worldwide. The Basilica of the National Shrine of the Immaculate Conception in Washington, D.C., is the largest Roman Catholic Church in North America.

Beatific Vision

In Exodus 33:20 our awesome God says that no one can see him and live. But that is while we are on earth. The Beatific Vision is beholding God face-to-face in **Heaven**. There we will no longer need faith. The Beatific Vision will bring us great joy that will last forever.

Beatitudes

Beatitudes are teachings of Jesus that lead to blessedness, or happiness. Each one is a value paired with a wonderful promise related to God's **kingdom**. Living the Beatitudes makes us Christlike.

Here are the Beatitudes:

Blessed are the poor in spirit, for theirs is the kingdom of Heaven.
Blessed are those who mourn, for they will be comforted.
Blessed are the meek, for they will inherit the earth.
Blessed are those who hunger and thirst for righteousness, for
    they will be filled.
Blessed are the merciful, for they will receive mercy.
Blessed are the pure in heart, for they will see God.
Blessed are the peacemakers, for they will be called children
    of God.

Blessed are those who are persecuted for righteousness' sake, for
theirs is the kingdom of Heaven.

Blessed are you when people revile you and persecute you and
utter all kinds of evil against you falsely on my account.

Rejoice and be glad, for your reward is great in Heaven.

bell

A church bell is a **sacramental**. It is rung to call people to worship and
to remind them about God. It is also rung at funerals and on special
occasions. Some churches ring bells at morning, noon, and evening
hours when it was customary to pray the **Angelus**. Small bells are
sometimes rung at Mass by altar servers during the Institution Narrative (formerly the **Consecration**) to call our attention to the presence
of Jesus in the sacred bread and wine.

Benediction

Benediction is a devotion to Jesus in the **Blessed Sacrament**. It occurs
after the Blessed Sacrament has been placed in a **monstrance** and
adored for a period of time. During Benediction the Blessed Sacrament is incensed and prayers are prayed. Then the celebrant wraps a
long scarf, called the humeral veil, around him and covers his hands
with it. He lifts the monstrance and makes the Sign of the Cross over
the people. We sing songs about the Eucharist and usually pray the
Divine Praises.

Bible

The Bible, or Sacred Scripture, is a collection of sacred books in which
God reveals himself as a loving, saving God and speaks to us. The
Holy Spirit inspired human writers to write the words, but God is the
author. This same Spirit guides the Church in interpreting what was
written.

Like a library, the Bible contains different kinds of writing: historical records, prophecies, short stories, prayers, proverbs, and songs.

The first forty-six books in the Bible are the Old Testament. It begins with the story of Creation and relates the history of the Jews, the people God chose to carry out his plan of Salvation. The Old Testament paves the way for and prophesies Christ. The New Testament is composed of 27 books. It opens with the **Gospels**, which tell about Jesus, the promised Savior. These are followed by the Acts of the Apostles, a book about the early years of his Church; many letters, mostly by St. Paul; and a prophetic book that shows the final triumph of goodness. The Church decided which books to accept in the canon, or official list, of biblical books. Catholic Bibles have more books than Protestant bibles and Jewish bibles. The additional ones, called deuterocanonical books, are Tobit, Judith, Wisdom, Sirach, Baruch, and 1 and 2 Maccabees. Catholic Bibles also include more text in the Books of Esther and Daniel.

At every Mass we hear readings from the Bible during the Liturgy of the Word. It nourishes and guides our Christian lives. The Bible was originally written in Hebrew and Greek. The *New American Bible* is the English translation used in our liturgies today. Every Catholic home should have a Bible. It's said that a person whose Bible is falling apart usually isn't! What does that mean?

bishop

A bishop is a successor of the **Apostles** and an overseer of the Church. He has the fullness of priesthood and can administer all the sacraments. Only a bishop can consecrate bishops and ordain priests and deacons. A bishop is a shepherd who usually cares for people within a **diocese** assisted by priests and deacons. His role is to teach, govern, and sanctify people. Like a shepherd, a bishop carries a staff called a **crosier**. He also wears a large pectoral cross, a special ring, and a **miter** (a tall, pointed hat). A bishop may wear purple garments. Every bishop has his own personally selected coat of arms and motto. The bishop's church in a diocese is called a **cathedral**. The bishop who leads a large or historically important diocese is an archbishop, and his diocese is an archdiocese.

All bishops work together with the pope as a "college" and meet occasionally in councils and synods. United States bishops belong to the United States Conference of Catholic Bishops (USCCB), which has its headquarters in Washington, D.C. They meet twice a year. Forms of the word *episcopacy* refer to bishops.

blasphemy

Blasphemy is the sin of insulting or showing contempt for God by word or deed. It includes showing contempt for the saints and persons or things consecrated to God.

Blessed

See **canonization**.

Blessed Sacrament

The Blessed Sacrament is the **Eucharist**. This name refers in particular to the sacred host reserved in the **tabernacle** for adoration and for taking to those who are sick. Because God is present in Catholic churches, we genuflect or bow toward the tabernacle and act with reverence there. We visit Jesus in the Blessed Sacrament when we can, and we make a **holy hour** before the Blessed Sacrament. The sacred host is displayed for **Benediction** and for **Forty Hours Devotion**.

blessing

1) A blessing is a favor from God that shows his love for us. For example, to be alive is a blessing.

2) When we say, "Blessed be God," we mean "God be praised" or "Thanks be to God."

3) A blessing is the **sacramental** of asking God to favor a person, place, or object. A blessing may also make something holy for a religious purpose; for example, by blessing water, a priest makes it sacred.

The blessing may be imparted by outstretched hands, the laying on of hands, sprinkling with holy water, or making the **Sign of the Cross** over the person or thing being blessed. **Laypeople** (those who are not ordained) may give blessings. The book *Catholic Household Blessings and Prayers*, published by the USCCB, contains many blessings useful for families, such as a blessing before leaving on a journey, a blessing for a birthday, and a blessing for times of trouble. Some parents bless their children every night.

Book of the Gospels
At Mass the Gospel is proclaimed from the Book of the Gospels. In the procession during the Entrance Chant, the **lector** carries this book slightly raised and places it on the altar. Later the priest processes to the **ambo** with the book to proclaim the Gospel. He may be accompanied by altar servers carrying candles and **incense**.

brother
A brother is a man consecrated to God who lives in community and follows the rule of a certain religious congregation. He makes **vows**, usually of poverty, chastity, and obedience. A brother's life is devoted to prayer and to serving the world in various **ministries**. He is not a priest, but there may be ordained men in his community.

C

Calvary
Calvary is the hill outside the walls of old Jerusalem on which Jesus died for us. *Calvary* is from the Latin word for "skull." In the Bible, Calvary is called Golgotha, which is "skull" in the language that Jesus spoke. Perhaps the hill looked like a skull. Some people think that the skull of **Adam** is buried there. Today inside the Basilica of the Holy Sepulcher in Jerusalem, visitors can view the rock of Calvary behind glass windows and touch it through a hole under the altar.

canon law

Every organization has laws. Canon law is the body of laws that govern the Catholic Church. The word *canon* is from the Greek word for "rule." Canon laws assure that the society of the Church runs smoothly. Pope John XXIII called for a revision of the *Code of Canon Law* on the same day that he called for the **Second Vatican Council**. This revision was published in 1983. Canon lawyers study canon law and earn degrees in it.

canonization

Canonization is the Church's declaration that a person is in Heaven and may be honored and imitated. The person is added to the canon, or list, of official saints. In the early years of the Church, martyrs were automatically considered saints. Since 1234, the pope has canonized saints. Declaring someone a saint is a long process. First, it must be proved that the person had heroic virtue or was a **martyr**. The local **bishop** collects and sends evidence to Rome. While the person's life is being investigated, he or she has the title Servant of God. If the group in charge of the causes of saints accepts the evidence, a biography of the candidate is written and studied. Experts may approve the cause and send it to the pope. If he approves, the person is declared Venerable. Then if a miracle is worked through the candidate's prayers, the pope beatifies him or her, and the person is called Blessed. After more study and another miracle, the pope may declare the person a **Saint**. A great celebration is usually held in St. Peter's Basilica in Rome. No miracles are required for martyrs.

canticle

A canticle is a sung prayer. The Gospel of Luke gives us three canticles that are prayed in the **Liturgy of the Hours**. They are the Canticle of Mary (the Magnificat) in Luke 1:46–55, the Canticle of Zechariah (Benedictus) in Luke 1:68–79, and the Canticle of Simeon (Nunc

Dimittis) in Luke 2:29–32. Their Latin titles are from their opening words. Canticles are also found in the Old Testament, for example, the Canticle of Moses in Deuteronomy 32:1–43.

Capital sins

Capital sins are bad moral habits that lead to other sins. They are also called vices or deadly sins. The traditional seven Capital sins are pride, envy, sloth (laziness), lust (an extraordinary desire for pleasure), greed, gluttony, and anger.

Capital virtues

The Capital virtues are the opposite of **Capital sins**. They lead to **holiness**. They are chastity (purity), temperance (self-control), charity, diligence (hard work), patience, kindness, and humility.

cardinal

A cardinal is a Church official who ranks next to the **pope** and is considered a prince of the Church. He is a **bishop** who has been appointed a cardinal by the pope and belongs to the College of Cardinals. Cardinals assist the pope in governing the Church. They are the heads of departments in the **Roman Curia**. Cardinals who are younger than age eighty are responsible for electing a new pope. A cardinal receives a gold ring from the pope and may wear red garments. Today there are about two hundred cardinals.

Cardinal Virtues

A virtue is a good habit or power. The word *cardinal* comes from the Latin for "hinge." The Cardinal Virtues are the four central virtues that other virtues depend on as a door depends on its hinges. The Cardinal Virtues are the source of or influence all other virtues. They are prudence (right judgment), justice (fairness, respecting rights), temperance (self-control), and fortitude (courage to do what is right).

cassock

A cassock is the long robe that is the official clothing of altar servers, priests, and bishops. Servers wear black, red, or white cassocks. Priests traditionally wear black cassocks, but in tropical climates they may wear white cassocks. Bishops may wear a purple cassock or a black one with touches of purple. Cardinals may wear a red cassock or a black one with touches of red. The pope's cassock has been white ever since the time of Pope Saint Pius V, who belonged to the Dominican order and wore a white **habit**.

catacomb

The early Christians, who believed in the **resurrection** of the body, called the catacombs "sleeping places." A catacomb is an underground system of tunnels and small rooms that were burial places for the first Christians, mainly in Rome. Some passageways run on top of one another. The graves were carved out of the walls horizontally, sometimes stacked three or four up a high wall. Ancient Christian art is found in the catacombs. Graves of some **martyrs** there became shrines. Today a few of the forty-some catacombs in Rome are open to the public.

catechism

A catechism is a book that presents Catholic **doctrine**. The *Catechism of the Catholic Church* is the primary catechism. It has four parts: the **Creed, liturgy, commandments,** and **prayer.** Religion textbooks used in schools must be in line with the truths in this catechism. Older catechisms presented the faith in the form of questions and answers. Now our official catechism explains what we believe in an interesting way, aided by quotations from Scripture and the saints. Each section ends with summary points. Every Catholic family would increase its knowledge of the **faith** by having this book at home and reading it.

catechist

Your religion teacher is a catechist. A catechist is someone who instructs others in the **faith**. The word *catechesis* comes from the Greek word for "echo." Through catechists the Good News is passed down through the centuries.

catechumen

A catechumen is a person who is studying the **doctrines** and life of the Church with the goal of becoming a member. By intending to become a Catholic, a catechumen is already joined to the Church. Through **Baptism** he or she becomes fully united with us. You might have seen catechumens who are in the **Rite of Christian Initiation of Adults** (RCIA) leave Mass after the readings. They are leaving to receive instruction in the faith.

cathedral

A cathedral is the central church of a **diocese** and the church of its **bishop**. The word *cathedral* comes from the Latin word for "seat" or "chair." A chair is a symbol of authority. For example, we celebrate the Feast of the Chair of Saint Peter, meaning his authority. Cathedrals tend to be large, domed, and decorated with religious art. There are many beautiful cathedrals in Europe, such as the Cathedral of Our Lady of Chartres in France, which has 176 stained-glass windows.

Catholic

1) A Catholic is a person who is a member of the Catholic Church headed by the pope. Nearly one out of every four Americans identifies himself or herself as Catholic. There are more than one billion Catholics worldwide.

2) Catholic is a mark, or characteristic, of the Catholic Church. It means universal. That is, the Church has the fullness of Christ's presence and means of **Salvation**, and is open to everyone in the world.

Catholic Church

The Catholic Church is the community of believers that Jesus founded on the **Apostles** in the first century. They are united in their beliefs and celebrate seven **sacraments**. The pope, the Bishop of Rome, is the visible head of the Church, and he and the other bishops govern the Church. The headquarters of the Church is in Rome. The Church includes a Western **Rite** (Roman or Latin) and several Eastern Rites.

See Matthew 16:18–19 for the story of how Jesus plans to build the Church.

censer

A censer is the metal container that holds the coals on which **incense** is burned in worship. It hangs from a chain or chains so that it can be swung to release fragrant smoke into the air. Another name for a censer is thurible. The person who carries the thurible is called a thurifer.

chalice

A chalice is the sacred cup that holds the sacred wine, the Blood of Christ, at the **Eucharist**. Because of its special role, a chalice is usually made of precious material that is not easily broken and of good quality. A bishop **consecrates** a chalice with **Chrism**.

chancery

The chancery is the diocesan office that handles documents used in the government of the diocese and houses its written records. The official in charge of the chancery is called the chancellor.

chapel

A chapel is a building or room for prayer and the celebration of the **Eucharist**. Religious communities have chapels, and some churches have chapels for the reservation of the **Blessed Sacrament** or as **shrines**. The word *chapel* comes from the shrine where the cloak, or capa, of Saint Martin of Tours was preserved. Saint Martin cut his military cloak in two in order to share it with a beggar. Then in a dream Martin saw Jesus wearing the cloak.

chaplain

A chaplain is someone who gives pastoral care to a certain group of people. This care includes listening, counseling, supporting, and praying with people in need. In the past, a priest provided this care to groups such as a community of sisters, hospital patients, prisoners, or military personnel. Today **deacons** and **laypeople** can also carry out this ministry after they register in a clinical pastoral education program and fulfill its requirements.

chaplet

When you pray the **Rosary**, you are praying on a type of chaplet. A chaplet is a string of beads on which prayers are said. There are many chaplets in honor of Jesus or the saints. The Chaplet of Divine Mercy and the Chaplet of Saint Michael are two examples. Usually chaplets have fewer beads than the Rosary.

character

A character is the permanent spiritual mark left on a person upon receiving the **Sacraments** of Baptism, Confirmation, or Holy Orders. These sacraments may be celebrated only once. The character signifies that a person has a special relationship with Christ.

charism

A charism is a special gift or **grace** from the **Holy Spirit** for the good of the Church. Saint Paul lists some charisms in 1 Corinthians 12:8–10, namely, speaking wisdom, speaking knowledge, faith, healing, miracles, prophecy, discernment of spirits (knowing if something is from God), speaking in tongues, and interpreting tongues. Religious congregations have particular charisms that their members are known for, such as love of the poor or concern for the elderly.

charity

1) Charity, or love, is the **Theological Virtue** given at **Baptism** that enables us to love God above all and love others for the love of God. Saint Paul pointed out that the other Theological Virtues (faith and hope) exist in Heaven, but love is the strongest of the virtues.

2) Donating money or objects or doing things to help those in need is called charity.

See 1 Corinthians 13:1–13 for Saint Paul's description of love.

chasuble

A chasuble is the long, sleeveless outer garment worn by the presider at the **Eucharist**. It is a large oval piece of material with a hole for the head like a poncho. The word *chasuble* comes from *casula*, which means "little house," because originally it completely covered the person. Later the sides were cut away to free the arms. Chasubles come in **liturgical colors** to match the liturgical season or the feast celebrated. Like most priestly vestments, chasubles are blessed. They symbolize the **charity** the priest will practice as he serves God's people.

Chi-Rho

You have probably seen the Chi-Rho on vestments and in religious art. It is a symbol for Jesus made from the first letters of the Greek word for **Christ**. "Ch" is Chi (X) and "r" is Rho (P). The two Greek letters are printed on top of each other. It is said that before a battle at the Milvian Bridge in 312, the Roman Emperor Constantine saw a Chi-Rho in a vision. After praying to the one God, he won the battle, converted to Christianity, and made it the state religion of the Roman Empire.

Chrism

Chrism is a mixture of oil and perfume, such as balsam, that is used for anointing. It is a Greek word that means "anointing." A person is anointed with Chrism during Baptism, Confirmation (which Eastern Catholic churches call Chrismation), and Holy Orders. It is also used in the **consecration** of churches, **altars**, **chalices**, and **patens**. Usually on **Holy Thursday**, the bishop blesses the oil at a Chrism Mass and sends it to parishes in his diocese.

Christ

You might think that Christ is Jesus' last name, but it's not. In his day people didn't have last names. Originally, Christ was a title that meant **Messiah** or "anointed one." Jesus was known as the Christ. Gradually, Christ became part of the proper name of Jesus. The religion that began with him is called Christianity, and his followers are called **Christians**.

Christian

A Christian is someone who accepts the teachings of Jesus Christ, tries to live as he did, and belongs to his Church. The **Acts of the Apostles** tells us that the followers of Jesus were first called Christians in Antioch, a chief city of the Near East that is now in modern Turkey. Today about one-third of the world's population are Christians, and half of these are Roman Catholics.

Christmas

Christmas is the feast of the Nativity, the birth of **Jesus** Christ, our Savior. It is celebrated on December 25, which is nine months after the **Annunciation** of the Lord, March 25. The word *Christmas* is a combination of *Christ* and *Mass*. Many people like to go to midnight Mass on this feast. Accounts of the birth of Jesus are found in Luke 2:1–20 and Matthew 1:18–25. These are the sources of Christmas Nativity scenes and Christmas hymns.

Church

1) The Church is the community of all the people of God. It includes the faithful on earth, the poor souls in **Purgatory**, and the saints in **Heaven**. The Church is the Body of Christ. He is the head, and we are

the members. We share life like a vine and its branches. The Church was founded by Jesus, born on **Calvary**, and is guided by the Holy Spirit. Mary is the Mother of the Church. The Church is led by the successors of the **Apostles**: the pope in Rome and all the bishops. It has four distinguishing **marks**, or qualities: one, holy, catholic, and apostolic.

2) A church is the sacred building where Christians gather to worship. It usually has a cross at the top, may have a bell, and is ordinarily named for God or a saint.

Church year

See **liturgical year**.

ciborium

A ciborium is the sacred vessel that holds the **consecrated** hosts in the **tabernacle**. It is shaped like a large cup, has a lid, and is usually made from precious metal.

clergy

All ministers ordained through the Sacrament of Holy Orders are members of the clergy: **deacons**, **priests**, and **bishops**. Nonordained members of the Church are called the **laity** or **laypeople**. Secular priests and deacons are connected to a diocese and are under the direct authority of its bishop. Priests who belong to a religious community are under the authority of the leader of their community instead. Holy Orders last until death. However, a priest or a deacon may become a layperson again. In that case he can no longer exercise his Holy Orders. Only men can be members of the clergy.

colors, liturgical

Symbolic colors are used at **liturgies** for vestments and the cloths in the sanctuary. Here are the colors, what they symbolize, and when they are used:

- white (purity, joy, glory): feasts of Our Lord (except those related to his Passion) and Our Lady, Christmas and Easter, angels and most saints, John the Baptist, John the Evangelist, Chair of Saint Peter, and the Conversion of Saint Paul
- red (suffering, blood, love): Passion (Palm) Sunday, Good Friday, Pentecost, feasts of the Apostles and the Evangelists (except for John), and martyrs
- violet (preparation, sorrow, penance): Advent and Lent
- green (life, hope): Ordinary Time

Other liturgical colors that are optional:

- rose (joy): Third Sunday of Advent (Gaudete Sunday) and the Fourth Sunday in Lent (Laetare Sunday)
- white, violet, and black: funeral Masses and All Souls Day
- Gold may replace white, red, or green.

commandments

The Ten Commandments are not just ten suggestions. The commandments are the laws that we must follow to keep our **covenant** and preserve our friendship with God. In the Bible, God inscribed ten laws on two stone tablets and gave them to Moses on Mount Sinai. They are also called the Decalogue (Ten Words). The first three commandments have to do with our relationship with God. The other seven deal with our relationship with others. Jesus taught that the greatest commandment is to love God with our whole heart and soul and mind. He said that the second greatest commandment is to love our neighbor as we love ourselves. At the Last Supper, Jesus added a new commandment: love one another as I have loved you. By following the Ten Commandments, we show love and attain Heaven. Taking the commandments to heart helps us when we make an **examination of conscience**.

Here are the Ten Commandments:

1. I am the LORD your God. You shall not have other gods before me.
2. You shall not take the name of the Lord your God in vain.
3. Remember to keep holy the Sabbath day.
4. Honor your father and your mother.
5. You shall not kill.
6. You shall not commit adultery.
7. You shall not steal.
8. You shall not bear false witness against your neighbor.
9. You shall not covet your neighbor's wife.
10. You shall not covet your neighbor's goods.

Commandments of the Church
See **Precepts of the Church.**

Communion
Communion is the body and blood of **Jesus** under the form of bread and wine. Unleavened (without yeast) bread called hosts and wine become the Body and Blood of Jesus at Mass through the words of the priest and the power of the **Holy Spirit**. Jesus is totally present in both the sacred bread and the sacred wine. Catholics who are free from **mortal sin** can receive Communion. We should **fast** from food and drink—not including water or medicine—for an hour before receiving Communion.

To receive the sacred host, we set our left hand on top of our right hand and bow. The sacred host is offered to us with the words "The body of Christ," and we respond, "Amen." Once the sacred host is in our hand, we step aside and place the host in our mouth with our right hand. We can choose to receive the sacred host on our tongue instead. The sacred wine is offered with the words "The blood of Christ," and we again respond, "Amen." We take a sip and return to our place.

Then we quietly talk to Jesus and pray prayers of adoration, thanksgiving, contrition, and love. We also join in the Communion song. Jesus is present within us in this special way as long as the sacred bread and wine have the characteristics of bread and wine. Receiving Communion makes us one with Jesus and one with everyone else who receives him. Through this gift our sins are forgiven, and our spiritual life grows.

Communion of Saints

1) In the Apostles' **Creed** we say that we believe in the Communion of Saints. By this we mean the union of the saints in **Heaven**, the souls in **Purgatory**, and the faithful on earth. We are all bound together in the Body of Christ. The three groups are sometimes called the Church triumphant, the Church suffering, and the Church militant (those still struggling to resist sin). We can ask the saints to pray for us, and we can pray for the people in Purgatory.

2) The Communion of Saints can also refer to the holy things that stand for and bring about our unity, especially the Eucharist.

conclave

A conclave is the enclosed meeting of **cardinals** for the purpose of electing a **pope**. The word *conclave* comes from the Latin for "with a key." During a conclave the cardinals are locked in. They do not have any contact with the outside world. All cardinals who are younger than age eighty gather in the Vatican's Sistine Chapel. A pope must be elected by a two-thirds majority. If no one has been elected after thirty votes, a simple majority is sufficient. After each vote, the ballots are burned, and the large crowd gathered outside can see the smoke. When a new pope has been chosen, chemicals are added to the fire to produce white smoke. This signals the world that the Catholic Church has a new Holy Father.

Confirmation

Confirmation is the second **Sacrament** of Initiation. It confirms, or strengthens, what occurred at **Baptism**. At Confirmation our relationship with Jesus deepens, the **Gifts of the Holy Spirit** are increased, and we take on more responsibility for witnessing to Jesus. A **bishop** is the ordinary minister of Confirmation. (At the Easter Vigil, when Baptism takes place, a priest may also confirm people.) The bishop states a person's Confirmation name, which may be the same as the baptismal name. Then with **Chrism** he traces a cross on the person's forehead and says, "(*Name*), be sealed with the gift of the Holy Spirit." In doing so, the bishop lays his hand over the person. The bishop prays a prayer asking God to increase the seven **Gifts of the Holy Spirit**. The person being confirmed has a sponsor, who is a practicing Catholic charged with fostering the person's faith. In the Eastern Catholic Church, Confirmation (called Chrismation) and First **Eucharist** are celebrated at the time the person is baptized.

conscience

After we sin, our conscience bothers us. Conscience is the power of our mind to judge an action as right or wrong. It is an internal sense that tells us the right thing to do. Knowledge of Church teaching makes for a correct conscience. We form a good conscience by learning about Church teachings and by associating with good people. Following a properly formed conscience leads to a good life.

consecration

1) Consecration is the setting aside of a person or an object for God and his service. For example, men and women religious are consecrated to God.

2) The part of the Mass when the bread and wine become the Body and Blood of Christ—through the words of the priest, the action of Christ, and the power of the Holy Spirit—is called the Consecration

or Institution Narrative. The key words of consecration are the same at every Mass. They are the words that Jesus spoke at the **Last Supper** when he instituted the **Eucharist**.

contemplation

Contemplation is the highest form of prayer and a gift from God. It is simply being aware of God and enjoying his presence. No words are spoken, but our hearts are filled with wonder and love. Saint Gregory the Great defined contemplation as "deep knowledge of God impregnated with love" and "resting in God."

contrition

Contrition is sorrow for sin coupled with the intention not to sin again. Contrition is required for our sins to be forgiven. In the Sacrament of **Penance**, we pray the Act of Contrition.

convent

A convent is ordinarily the house or building where women religious live. It can also mean the house of men religious. The word *monastery* is used instead of *convent* to refer to the homes of some religious communities.

corporal

During Mass the priest opens a folded piece of white linen and spreads it on the altar. He places the sacred hosts and chalice on it. That white material is a corporal, an altar linen that has been blessed. It is used to catch any crumbs from the host during **liturgies** that involve the Blessed Sacrament. The word *corporal* comes from the Latin word for "body." A corporal is at least fifteen inches square and folded in nine parts. It may have a cross sewn on the edge nearest the priest and may be trimmed in lace.

Corporal Works of Mercy

See **Works of Mercy**.

covenant

A covenant is a solemn agreement between people or between people and God. Another word for covenant is "testament." The **Old Testament** tells of three main covenants. First, God promised Noah that he would never again destroy the world by flood, and human beings were to respect and care for living things. Second, God promised **Abraham** many descendants and the land of Canaan. In return, all males would be circumcised. Third, at Mount Sinai, the Israelites promised to obey God, and God said that they would be his special people. In the **New Testament**, at the **Last Supper**, Jesus spoke of the New Covenant established by his blood. We are people of this New Covenant. It will be fulfilled at the end of time.

credence table

The credence table is the side table in the **sanctuary** that holds the **chalice**, **paten**, **cruets**, and other items needed for Mass. It is usually covered with a white cloth.

creed

At Sunday Masses we stand and pray a creed. A creed is a statement of faith in which beliefs are listed. The word *creed* comes from the Latin for "I believe." The two most familiar creeds are the Apostles' Creed, which summarizes the teachings of the Apostles, and the **Nicene Creed**. These creeds are prayed not only by Roman Catholics but by most Christian churches.

crosier

A crosier is the staff carried by a **bishop** at **liturgies** as a sign of his authority. It has a hook at the top to resemble a shepherd's crook. A bishop is the shepherd, or pastor, of the Church, Christ's flock.

cross

1) It's strange that Christians wear crosses around their necks considering that the cross is an instrument of execution. In the Roman Empire, criminals who weren't Roman citizens were tied by ropes or nailed to a cross until they died. This was the punishment for rebellion and served as warning to people. Jesus sacrificed his life for us on a cross and turned it into a sign of victory. That is why the cross is the symbol of the Christian **faith**. The **apostle Peter** was crucified upside down, and the apostle Andrew was killed on an X-shaped cross. The usual cross is the Latin T-shaped cross. Different kinds of crosses have different meanings. For example, the Orthodox cross has two additional bars, one bar for the INRI sign and one for the footrest.

We celebrate the feast of the Exaltation, or Triumph of the Cross, on September 14. On Good Friday we participate in the **veneration** of the cross. A short prayer you might adopt is "We adore you, O Christ, and we praise you, because by your holy cross, you have redeemed the world."

2) Suffering in our lives is called a cross. Jesus told us to take up our cross and follow him. We can unite our suffering with that of Jesus and in a small way, participate in his redeeming suffering. We can offer up our crosses to God for an intention, such as a grace for a friend or for world peace.

crucifix

Not every **cross** is a crucifix. A crucifix is a cross that bears the image of Jesus. Usually above his head is a sign with **INRI**, the initials of his "crime": Jesus, King of the Jews. At Mass, where the sacrifice of Jesus is re-presented, a crucifix is always on or near the **altar**. A traditional prayer people sometimes pray after Communion is The Prayer before a Crucifix.

See John 19:16–37 for the story of the Crucifixion of Jesus.

cruet

A cruet is a sacred vessel that holds the water or wine used at Mass. Cruets may be made of glass and have a stopper. The wine and water are usually brought to the altar in a procession with the hosts during the Presentation and Preparation of the Gifts.

Crusades

The Crusades were military expeditions undertaken by Western Europeans to keep the Holy Land out of the hands of Muslims. Eight major expeditions occurred between 1096 and 1270. The word *crusade* comes from the crosses that crusaders wore and carried on pennants. The Crusades were proclaimed by **popes** and promoted by saints. They had both good and bad effects. In the end they were not successful.

D

David

As Jesus entered Jerusalem, people saluted him as the son of David and spread palm branches before him. David, who lived from about 1040 to 970 BC, was the greatest king of Israel. He united the northern and southern tribes into one nation. When David was a shepherd boy, the youngest of Jesse's eight sons, God sent the **prophet** Samuel to **anoint** him as future king. As a young man, David soothed King Saul by playing the lyre, a kind of harp. In a battle with the Philistines, David killed the giant Goliath with a stone from a slingshot. David's success in war and growing popularity made Saul so jealous that he tried to kill David more than once. Saul's daughter Michal, who was David's wife, and later Saul's son, Jonathan, who was David's friend, helped David escape.

Saul and Jonathan died in battle, and David became king. David united the northern and southern kingdoms of Israel and brought the Ark of the Covenant to Jerusalem. Unfortunately, David sinned by arranging to have a neighbor, a soldier, killed in war so he could marry the man's wife, Bathsheba. But then David repented. He is credited with writing the **psalms**. His son Solomon succeeded him on the throne.

deacon

You might mistake a deacon for a priest because deacons may wear Roman collars. A deacon is a man who has been ordained to the first level of priesthood called the diaconate. He assists the bishops and priests and devotes himself to works of **charity**. The word *deacon* comes from the Greek word for servant. A transitional deacon is a deacon for a short time as a step in preparing to become a priest. A permanent deacon is a deacon for life. A permanent deacon must be at least thirty-five years old. He may be married before he becomes a permanent deacon, but he cannot marry after he is ordained.

A deacon may perform Baptisms, assist the priest during **liturgies**, proclaim the Gospel and preach at Mass, assist at and bless marriages, and preside at funerals. At liturgies a deacon wears a **stole** draped over his left shoulder and across his chest. The story of the choosing of the first deacons is in Acts of the Apostles 6:1–6. The first martyr was a deacon named Stephen. Saint Lawrence is another deacon-martyr. In the early Church, some women called deaconesses served the Church in various ways, but there is no evidence that they were ordained.

Dead Sea Scrolls

In 1947, a shepherd made an amazing discovery. In a cave he found the first set of Dead Sea Scrolls. Sometime around the first century the scrolls were stored in jars and placed in eleven caves on the shore of the Dead Sea. The scrolls, which are mostly in Hebrew, are thought to be the library of a Jewish religious community at Qumran called the Essenes. They contain at least fragments of almost every **Old**

Testament book and other works, including a rule book for a community. Today the scrolls are housed in the Shrine of the Book in Jerusalem.

Decalogue
See **commandments**.

Deposit of Faith
The Deposit of Faith is the treasure of **faith** revealed in **Scripture** and **Tradition** and handed down by the **Apostles**. It is the complete collection of truths taught and interpreted by the Church.

desert fathers/mothers
The desert fathers and mothers were **hermits** who lived in an Egyptian desert in about the late third century. They lived a life of solitude, self-denial, and prayer as monks and nuns. Their strict, holy way of life inspired the formation of monasteries. The most famous desert father is Saint Anthony the Hermit.

devil
In art the devil wears a red suit, has horns, and carries a pitchfork. In the real world, the devil is invisible. The devil, or Satan, is a fallen **angel**, a pure and mighty spirit who turned against God. The Bible tells of a war in which the devils were conquered by the faithful angels who were led by the archangel Michael. The consequence for the devils was separation from God forever, which is **Hell**. Scripture relates that Satan caused the fall of the human race. He lied to our first parents and tempted them to disobey God, their creator and friend. They gave in to temptation. This led to the loss of God's friendship, suffering, and death.

In the Gospels, Jesus showed power over Satan by casting devils out of people. Today certain priests perform **exorcisms** to free people who are possessed by the devil. Jesus saved us from the Evil One by his death on the **cross**. The devils' hatred for God impels them to tempt us to turn against God. Each time we pray the **Our Father**, we ask God to deliver us from evil, meaning the Evil One.

See Matthew 4:1–11 for the story of Jesus being tempted by the devil.

devil's advocate

In the process of **canonization**, an official is appointed to argue against the proposed saint's holiness or miracle. This objector is known as a devil's advocate. An advocate is a lawyer, a person who speaks on behalf of someone.

Didache (DID-ah-kay)

The Didache, or The Teaching of the Twelve Apostles, is a Christian **catechism** from the first century. It covers Christian **morality**, **liturgy**, and the life of the early Christian community.

diocese

A diocese consists of the Catholics within a certain region under the authority of a bishop. It is divided into **parishes**. Some dioceses are not geographical but united by a certain **rite** or language. In the **Eastern Churches**, a diocese is called an eparchy. A military diocese encompasses military personnel and their families. A large or historically important diocese is known as an archdiocese and is led by an archbishop.

disciple

A disciple is a student and follower of a certain teacher who is usually referred to as a master. In this sense, all of us who are baptized are disciples of Jesus, the Master. In the Bible the word *disciples* referred to the **Apostles** and the seventy-two followers of Jesus who were sent out to preach.

Divine Office

See **Liturgy of the Hours**.

Divine Providence

See **Providence, Divine**.

Doctor of the Church

In addition to medical doctors, there are doctors who have a Ph.D. in a particular subject. For Catholics, "Doctor of the Church" is a title given to more than thirty saints whose writings or teachings on the faith are considered outstanding. The first four Doctors of the Church were Gregory the Great, Ambrose, Augustine, and Jerome. There are also women who were named Doctors of the Church: Catherine of Siena, Teresa of Avila, Thérèse of Lisieux, and Hildegard of Bingen.

doctrine

A doctrine is all the truths found in Divine Revelation (**Scripture** and **Tradition**) and taught by the **Catholic Church** as necessary to believe. A single one of these truths is also called a doctrine. The *Catechism of the Catholic Church* presents and explains our doctrine.

dogma

A dogma is a solemnly defined teaching of the **Church** to be believed by all. This teaching is either revealed clearly in **Scripture** or **Tradition**, or it is implied. For example, the Immaculate Conception of Mary is dogma, although it is not explicitly stated in Scripture that she was sinless from the moment of her conception.

doxology

A doxology is a prayer in which we praise and give glory to God. The Greater Doxology is the Gloria of the **Mass**. The Lesser Doxology is the prayer Glory Be to the Father.

E

Easter

What is the greatest feast of all in the Church? No, it's not Christmas; it's Easter. Easter is also the oldest feast in the Church. On Easter we celebrate the **Resurrection** of Jesus. By rising from the tomb with a new and glorious life, Jesus triumphed over death. He led us from the slavery of sin to new life. At the Easter Vigil Mass (held the night before Easter) the **Paschal (Easter) Candle** is lit and carried through the dark church. People hold candles and pass the light of Christ to one another. The "Exsultet," an ancient Easter hymn, is sung. Several Scripture passages that trace Salvation History are read, water is blessed, and **catechumens** are baptized. All present renew their baptismal promises. The Easter season lasts fifty days and ends with Pentecost. During this time, the Paschal Candle is lit at each Mass, and alleluias are said and sung repeatedly.

On Easter morning some people like to view the sunrise, which is a symbol of the risen Son. Other objects associated with Easter are symbolic. New life is represented by flowers, green grass, and rabbits (which are prolific). Eggs from which chicks emerge represent the tomb from which Christ came out with new life. The Easter lily is shaped like a trumpet as if heralding the glory of the Resurrection. It is white, which stands for purity, and gold, the color of glory and royalty.

Easter Candle

See **Paschal Candle**.

Easter Triduum

The prefix *tri* means "three," as in tricycle, a bike with three wheels. The Easter Triduum, also called the Holy Triduum, is the three-day period that begins on **Holy Thursday** with the Mass of the Lord's Supper, includes **Good Friday** and **Holy Saturday**, and ends with evening prayer on Easter Sunday. It is the high point of the Church year, for it celebrates the Passion, Death, and **Resurrection** of Jesus.

Eastern Churches

At first there were five main Christian Churches, or **patriarchates**: Jerusalem, Antioch, Alexandria, and Constantinople (Byzantium), in the East, and Rome in the West. In 1054, the Great Schism occurred, and the Eastern Churches separated from the Western Church. These Eastern Churches are called Orthodox. They developed liturgies and spiritualities based on certain cultures. With time, some groups within the Eastern Churches reunited with Rome. They include the Byzantine, Coptic, Ethiopian, Chaldean, Melkite, Maronite, Syrian, and Armenian. Except for the Maronite, all of these have Orthodox counterparts. Eastern Churches are known for their emphasis on the glory and mystery of God and for their **icons.**

ecumenical council (EH-kyoo-MEN-ih-kul)

An ecumenical council is an assembly of **bishops** from all over the world called by the **pope** to discuss and make decisions concerning doctrine and Christian life. It is the highest teaching authority in the Church. There have been twenty-one ecumenical councils. The first one was the Council of Nicea in 325. The last one was the **Second Vatican Council** (Vatican II), which met from 1962 to 1965. Pope John XXIII called this council in order to open the windows of the Church and let in fresh air—in other words, to modernize it.

Ecumenism (eh-KYOO-muh-nizm)

Jesus prayed that his **Church** may be one. Ecumenism is the movement to reconcile **Christian** churches: Catholic, Orthodox, and Protestant. Members of different Christian churches meet to discuss the **theology** and history that has split Christ's Church. The hope is that someday all Christians will be united. Each year since 1908, the

Week of Prayer for Christian Unity has been observed from January 18 through 25.

Eden

In the Bible, Eden was a beautiful garden in the East where God placed the first people, **Adam** and **Eve**. There they enjoyed happiness and immortality (living forever). After our first parents sinned, they were banished from this garden. Then God placed cherubim (winged angels) and a flaming sword in Eden to guard the tree of life. Eden had many trees and a river with four branches, which included the Tigris and Euphrates Rivers in ancient Mesopotamia. Another name for Eden is Paradise.

Emmanuel

Emmanuel is a title for Jesus that means "God with us." The name Emmanuel is fitting for Jesus because he is God made flesh. In Matthew 1:22–23 a verse from the **prophet** Isaiah is applied to Jesus: "Behold, the virgin shall be with child and bear a son, and they shall name him Emmanuel" (Isaiah 7:14). During Advent we sing the hymn "O Come, O Come, Emmanuel," which is the **O Antiphons** set to music.

encyclical (en-SIK-lih-kul)

An encyclical is a long, formal letter from the **pope** about a matter of **faith**. An encyclical's title comes from its opening words in Latin. For example, Pope Benedict XVI's first encyclical was *Deus Caritas Est*, which means "God is love." An encyclical is intended for the whole Church or whole world.

Epiphany (ee-PIH-fuh-nee)

1) An epiphany is a manifestation of God, that is, God showing himself.

2) Epiphany is the feast that commemorates the **Magi's** visit to the infant Jesus. Because the Magi were not Jews, the feast marks the epiphany, or revelation, of Jesus to the Gentiles. Jesus is the Savior of both Jews and **Gentiles**, the whole world. The Magi paid homage to the newborn king and presented him with gifts of gold, frankincense, and myrrh. In the United States, the Epiphany is celebrated on the Sunday between January 2 and January 8. At different times and in different Churches, other epiphanies were celebrated on the Feast of the Epiphany, such as Jesus' baptism by John the Baptist and the miracle at Cana.

A custom on the Epiphany is to bless a house and mark its doorways with chalk. A family leader writes the initials of the Magi's traditional names (Caspar, Melchior, Balthazar) between the first two and last two digits of the current year with crosses dividing the symbols. For example, 20 + C + M + B + 14.

epistle

An Epistle is one of the twenty-one letters in the **New Testament**. The Epistles deal with problems in the new Christian churches, clarify **theology**, and exhort the Christians to live the Gospel. The letter usually opens with a greeting and thanksgiving to God. The body includes teaching, discussion of Christian behavior, and practical matters. The epistle closes with greetings, instructions to individuals, and a blessing.

Most of the Epistles were written by Saint **Paul** or his followers to the early Christian communities. They were usually named for the recipients. Ephesians, Philippians, Colossians, and Philemon are called captivity letters because Paul wrote them from jail. First and Second Timothy and Titus, named for the recipients, are called pastoral letters because they advise these two bishops. Seven letters are named for their authors and are catholic (universal) because they are letters to all Christians. They are James; First and Second Peter; First, Second, and

Third John; and Jude. The Second Reading at Mass is usually taken from one of the Epistles.

eschatology (EHSS-kuh-TAHL-uh-jee)

Eschatology is the teaching about the end times, or what is known as the four last things: death, judgment, Heaven, and Hell. For Christians, the culmination of God's plan of Salvation is the parousia, the second coming of Christ. On that day, the world as we know it will give way to the **Kingdom of God**. The dead will rise, and all humankind will be judged. According to Jesus, no one but the Father knows the day when the world will end.

Essenes

Essenes are Jewish men who lived in desert communities and city groups. They tried to live pure lives, doing **penance** and waiting for the coming of God. They existed from the second century BC to the first century AD. It is thought that the Essenes produced the **Dead Sea Scrolls**, which were discovered at Qumran in 1947. Some people think that Saint **John the Baptist** was an Essene.

eternal life

Fairy tales often end with the phrase "and they lived happily ever after." Eternal life is just that: living happily ever after. It refers to the unending and full life that human beings will enjoy if they die in a state of friendship with God. This was the destiny that God originally planned for us. But as a consequence of the sin of **Adam** and **Eve**, we could no longer hope for eternal life. Then our good and merciful God sent his Son to become man, suffer, die, and rise to atone for our sins. By doing so, Jesus won eternal life for us. He promises eternal life to those who believe in him and who eat the bread of life, the Eucharist.

See John 6:54–58 for Jesus' promise of eternal life.

eternity

Eternity is infinite time, which means having no beginning or end. God is eternal; he always was and always will be. For God, everything is now. In 2 Peter 3:8, we read, "But do not ignore this one fact, beloved, that with the Lord one day is like a thousand years and a thousand years like one day." The circle is a symbol for God because it has no beginning or end.

Eucharist (YOO-kar-ist)

1) The Eucharist is the Body and Blood of Jesus Christ under the appearances of bread and wine. The change in substance, called **transubstantiation**, is brought about at Mass through the words of the priest, the action of Christ, and the power of the Holy Spirit. In the Eucharist, Jesus is offered to the Father at Mass, comes to us as spiritual food in Holy Communion, and remains with us in the tabernacle. It is the **Real Presence**.

2) The **Sacrifice** of the Mass is also called the Eucharist. The word *eucharist* is from the Greek for "thanksgiving." The Mass is our supreme act of thanksgiving. It is our chief act of worship in which the sacrifice of Jesus for our Salvation is re-presented. We offer ourselves to the Father with him. Jesus instituted the Eucharist at the Last Supper as a memorial of his Death and **Resurrection**. The four main parts of the Eucharist are the Introductory Rites, the Liturgy of the Word, the Liturgy of the Eucharist, and the Concluding Rites.

3) The Eucharist is one of the **Sacraments** of Initiation. Through the Eucharist we become one with Jesus and with his Church.

evangelical counsels

The evangelical counsels are good actions that were taught and practiced by Jesus in the Gospels. They are poverty, chastity, and obedience. The counsels lead to the perfection of Christian life. Members of most religious institutes make public **vows** to live these counsels.

However, they are recommended for all people to practice according to their state in life.

Evangelist

1) Notice the word *angel* in *evangelist*. An angel is a messenger. An evangelist is a messenger too, someone who proclaims the Good News, the **Gospel**.

2) An Evangelist is one of the four authors of the Gospels: Matthew, Mark, Luke, and John. Their respective symbols as depicted in Christian art are a man, a lion, an ox, and an eagle. It is said that each symbol was chosen for the way the author's particular Gospel begins. Matthew's Gospel opens with the genealogy of Jesus. Mark's begins with John the Baptist roaring out his message. Luke's starts with Zechariah offering incense in the Temple of sacrifice. And John's begins with a lofty hymn about the Word before time.

evangelization

Evangelization is spreading the message about Jesus by word and example. Jesus commissioned his disciples to go out to all the world and tell the good news. Every Christian has the responsibility to evangelize and witness to Jesus. The three most recent popes have encouraged a New Evangelization. Its primary goal is to bring back Catholics who have left the Church.

Eve

Eve is the mother of all the living, the first woman. In the Bible, God created Eve from **Adam's** rib to be his partner. Tempted by **Satan**, Eve disobeyed God and then persuaded Adam to disobey too. This **Original Sin** affected the whole human race. Mary, the Mother of God, is called the new Eve because her Son saved us.

ex cathedra (EX KATH-eh-druh)

The expression *ex cathedra* is Latin for "from the chair." The "chair" represents authority. *Ex cathedra* describes solemn pronouncements of the **pope** that are infallible, or definitely true. For an *ex cathedra* **dogma**, the pope must speak as the supreme teacher of the Church with the authority as the successor of **Peter** on a matter of faith or morals. The dogma must be for the universal Church. Such pronouncements are very rare. The last dogma declared *ex cathedra* was the **Assumption** of Mary in 1950.

examination of conscience

An examination of conscience is the religious practice of reflecting on a period of our life to see how faithful we have been to God. The purpose is to root out sin and become a better, more loving Christian. We make an examination of conscience to prepare for the Sacrament of **Penance**. We pray to the **Holy Spirit** to help us make a good examination of conscience.

excommunication

Excommunication is the penalty of being separated from the **Church** and forbidden to share in its **sacraments** or **sacramentals**. It is the result of a very serious offense, such as heresy or physically attacking the pope. Some excommunications are decided by three judges in an official trial. Others are automatic.

Exodus

1) The Exodus is the great saving event of the **Old Testament** in which God, acting through **Moses**, led his people, the Israelites, out of slavery in Egypt. God made a **covenant** with them and gave them the promised land of Canaan. Jewish people recall and celebrate the Exodus every year at Passover, in particular at the Seder meal. The Exodus is a foreshadowing of Jesus' passing over to the Father through Death

and **Resurrection** to free us from sin. We celebrate this event in Salvation History at the banquet of the **Eucharist**.

2) The Book of Exodus is the second book in the Bible. It tells the story of the Exodus, God saving the Israelites from slavery in Egypt.

See Exodus 14:1–31 for the story of the Israelites escaping the Egyptians by crossing through the Red Sea.

exorcism

See **possession**.

exposition

Exposition is the ritual of placing the **Blessed Sacrament** on the altar for **adoration**. A large host is kept in a circular glass case called a luna. It is set in a large holder called a **monstrance** for all to see. Private or communal prayers are prayed. Some churches and chapels provide continual exposition with perpetual adoration. People sign up for a time during the day or night when they will be present to pray. Holy hours are commonly made with exposition.

extraordinary minister

An extraordinary minister is a person who has special permission to administer one of the **sacraments**. In an emergency, anyone may administer Baptism as an extraordinary minister. The ordinary minister of Confirmation is a bishop, but a priest may confirm in certain circumstances. **Laypeople** may be authorized by the bishop to distribute the Eucharist, usually after a training period. Being an extraordinary minister of the Eucharist is a beautiful way to serve the Church.

F

faith

1) Faith is the truths contained in **Revelation** and Church teachings. In a **creed** we state the chief truths of our faith and profess to believe them.

2) Faith is the virtue by which religious truths are believed. Faith is a gift, a **Theological Virtue** received at **Baptism**. It enables us to know God and everything that he has revealed. Faith also involves trusting God with all our heart in a special relationship. This aspect of faith is what we mean when we say we have faith in our doctor. Jesus healed people because of their faith and scolded his disciples when they didn't have it.

See Matthew 17:14–20, in which Jesus speaks about the power of faith.

Fall

See **Original Sin.**

fasting

Fasting is refraining from or limiting food or drink. Religious reasons for fasting are to show devotion to God, to do **penance**, and to practice self-control. Catholics age twenty-one to sixty are obliged to fast on **Ash Wednesday** and **Good Friday** by taking a main meal and two lesser meals that together are less than the main meal. We also fast from food and drink, including gum, for one hour before receiving Holy Communion. Before beginning his public ministry, Jesus fasted for forty days. Fasting is one of the three main Lenten practices. The others are prayer and **almsgiving.**

Father, God the

God the Father is the First Person of the Blessed **Trinity**. He is Father because God the Son is begotten of him. He is also the Father because we attribute to him the work of creation. He brought everything into existence. Jesus called him *Abba*, which means "Father." Jesus taught us to address his Father as "Father" in prayer when he gave us the Lord's Prayer.

Fathers of the Church

Fathers of the Church are saintly men who greatly influenced Church teaching and spread the faith before the middle of the eighth century. They accomplished this through writings, sermons, and their lives. Thirty-nine Fathers are Western (Latin), and forty-nine are Eastern (Greek). Those who lived at or near the same time as the Apostles are known as Apostolic Fathers. Some well-known Fathers of the Church are Gregory the Great, Justin Martyr, John Chrysostom, Basil, Ambrose, and Augustine.

First Fridays

See **Sacred Heart.**

fish

The study of fish is called ichthyology. *Ichthus* is the Greek word for fish. The fish logo you may have seen on decals and bumper stickers is a symbol for Jesus. This is because the initials of the Greek words for the phrase "Jesus Christ, Son of God, Savior" are ICHTHUS. It is thought that during persecutions, early Christians used the symbol of a fish to identify themselves to one another. Supposedly a Christian would draw one arc of a fish, and if the other person was Christian, he or she would draw the other arc to complete the secret symbol.

Forty Hours Devotion

Some churches carry on the tradition of holding Forty Hours Devotion. The **Blessed Sacrament** is exposed for forty hours and adored. The hours may be consecutive or broken up for security reasons. The forty hours refers to the time that Jesus spent in the tomb. This devotion originated in the sixteenth century. Saint John Neumann, bishop of Philadelphia, promoted it in the United States after he heard Jesus encouraging him to do so.

free will

God made us in his image and likeness. This means that we have an intellect with the power to think and a will with the power to choose. God does not force us to choose to do good. Neither can we say, "The devil made me do it." We are free to decide to obey God or not, to love or not. In other words, the choice is ours: eternal life with God or eternal separation from him.

See Deuteronomy 30:11–20 to read about choice and consequence.

Fruits of the Spirit

Jesus pointed out that a good tree bears good fruit (Matthew 7:17). His followers are to be known by the Fruits of the Spirit. These are the visible qualities that result from having a strong relationship with God and living a good Christian life. They are the first fruits of the glory we will have in Heaven. Tradition lists these twelve fruits: charity, joy, peace, patience, kindness, goodness, generosity, gentleness, faithfulness, modesty, self-control, and chastity. Nine of the fruits are found in Galatians 5:22–23.

G

Gabriel

Gabriel is one of the three **archangels**, or chief angels, who appear and are named in the Bible. Gabriel told the prophet Daniel the meaning of his visions. He also announced the birth of John the Baptist to his father Zechariah and the birth of Jesus to Mary. Some think that Gabriel was the unnamed angel who spoke to Joseph in dreams, who sent the shepherds to see the baby Jesus, and who comforted Jesus during his agony in the garden. There is a tradition that Gabriel will blow a trumpet to signal the end of the world. Muslims believe that the angel Gabriel dictated the Qu'ran to Muhammad. Saint Gabriel's feast day is September 29. Because of his role as messenger, Gabriel is the patron of communications and postal workers. The name Gabriel means "strength of God."

Galilee

Under the Roman occupation, Israel was divided into three provinces. Galilee was the northern province and the largest. Its inhabitants had a distinctive accent. Both Nazareth, the hometown of Jesus, and Capernaum, where he lived during his public life, are in Galilee. So, too, are the Sea of Galilee and Mount Tabor. According to the **Synoptic Gospels**, Jesus carried out most of his ministry in this province. Galilee was home to many **Gentiles**, crossed by a main trade route, and far from the Holy City of Jerusalem. For these reasons, other Jews looked down on Jews from Galilee, including Jesus, its most famous citizen.

Gehenna

Before the time of Jesus, in a valley outside **Jerusalem**, people sacrificed their children by fire to false gods. This valley was Gehenna. Jesus used the term for a place where the wicked who are not worthy of the Kingdom of God will suffer in fire forever. In some Bibles, Gehenna is translated as **Hell**.

general absolution

See **Penance**.

Genesis

Genesis is the first book of the Bible and of the **Pentateuch**. Its name is from the Greek for "origin," and its opening words are "In the beginning." This book includes the Jewish stories of the origin of the world, the human race, and the Jewish people. It appears to be woven from four different sources. After describing the creation of the world,

Genesis offers two accounts of the creation of man and woman. This is followed by the stories of Noah, **Abraham**, Isaac, and Jacob. Genesis concludes with the story of Jacob's son Joseph, through whom the Israelites are brought to Egypt.

Gentile

A Gentile is anyone who is not Jewish. Gradually, the early **Church** came to realize that it was meant not only for Jews but for Gentiles too. It took another step by deciding that Gentile converts did not need to follow Jewish customs. The **Holy Spirit** led **Peter** to see this with the help of **Paul**, who promoted the new concept. Paul's impressive work evangelizing Gentiles earned him the title of Apostle to the Gentiles.

genuflection

In church, people genuflect or bow. A genuflection, bending the right knee to the floor, is an act of reverence. To show respect for the **Blessed Sacrament**, we genuflect before entering a **pew** and after leaving it. On Christmas and on the Annunciation of the Lord, we genuflect during the **Creed** at the mention of the Incarnation. After the adoration of the cross on **Good Friday** until the Easter Vigil, we genuflect before the cross. At Mass the priest genuflects three times, but if the Blessed Sacrament is present in the tabernacle, he only genuflects before and after Mass.

A guide for how long to genuflect is the prayer "My Jesus, I adore you in the Sacrament of your love." Adopt the practice of saying this prayer as you genuflect.

Gethsemane (Geth-SEHM-uh-nee)

Gethsemane is the garden on the Mount of Olives where Jesus prayed after the **Last Supper**. It was there that Judas betrayed him and Jesus was captured. The name Gethsemane means "oil press." Today some very old olive trees still grow there, but not the ones from Jesus' time. Those were destroyed by the Romans.

gift of tongues

1) The gift of tongues, or glossolalia (GLAH-soh-LAY-lee-ah), is the ability to speak in a way that people who speak other languages can understand. The **Apostles** had this gift, or **charism**, on **Pentecost**.

2) Another form of the gift is being able to understand someone who is speaking in a foreign language.

3) The common meaning of the gift of tongues today is praying and speaking in unintelligible language. Some people in the charismatic movement possess this gift. Although the speaker may not understand the words, someone hearing them may have the gift of interpretation. In 1 Corinthians 14:1–25 Saint Paul pointed out that other gifts are more useful for the Church than the gift of tongues.

Gifts of the Holy Spirit

The Gifts of the Holy Spirit are **supernatural** dispositions or instincts that God gives to help us live as Jesus taught by responding to **graces**. They are listed in Isaiah 11:2. Jesus possessed these gifts in full. We receive them at **Baptism**, and they are increased at **Confirmation**.

These are the seven gifts:

- Wisdom: gives us the ability to contemplate divine mysteries
- Understanding: helps us grasp the meaning of the truths of our faith
- Counsel: helps us make good judgments and give good advice
- Fortitude (courage): gives us strength to endure trials, especially as we fulfill God's will
- Knowledge: helps us see everything and everyone from God's point of view
- Piety: enables us to regard God as a loving Father and to love him in return
- Fear of the Lord (wonder and awe): keeps us from sin out of respect for God's majesty

God

God is the supreme, perfect being who created all things. He is an uncreated spirit who is infinite, eternal, **omniscient**, **omnipotent**, **omnipresent**, and unchanging. We believe in one God who is a **Trinity** of Three Persons: Father, Son, and Holy Spirit. For us, God is personal, not just a force. The Bible states, "God is love" (1 John 4:16). God revealed his love for us in Scripture and especially in his Son, Jesus.

Reason leads us to realize that God exists. For example, the complexity, order, and beauty of creation point to an intelligent creator. Also, because everything has a cause, there must be One who caused things to begin. Because of who God is, we worship him. Where God is, Heaven is. There our all-holy God is surrounded by saints and **angels** who constantly give him glory.

godparents

Godparents are sponsors of a person being baptized. They are responsible for helping the infant or adult live a Christian life. A sponsor is also required for **Confirmation** and may be one of the godparents. Godparents must be practicing Catholics, at least sixteen years old, who have been confirmed. They must not be a parent of the person being baptized. Since only one Catholic godparent is required, a Christian who is not Catholic may serve as a witness.

Golden Rule

The Golden Rule is "Do to others whatever you would have them do to you." (Matthew 7:12) Jesus made this statement, which is also found in Jewish writings and is taught by most religions. The negative expression of this statement is the silver rule: "Do not do to others what you dislike having done to you."

Good Friday

Good Friday is the day of **Holy Week** and of the **Easter Triduum** when we remember and pray about the Death of Jesus. It is a day of fasting. Although there is no Mass on Good Friday, services are held in which Holy Communion is distributed. These services include the reading of the Passion according to John, special intercessions, and the veneration of the **cross** in which people file up to the cross and kiss it or show respect in another way. The altar is bare, and the priest wears red or black vestments. People may observe this holy day of mourning by praying the **Stations of the Cross** and by keeping silence.

Good News

See **Gospel**.

Good Shepherd

Jesus called himself the Good Shepherd who lays down his life for his sheep. (John 10:1–2) He explained that he is a personal shepherd, one who calls his sheep by name. His love impelled him to sacrifice his life for his sheep. He is not like a hired hand who runs away and leaves the sheep alone when a wolf threatens them. Moreover, Jesus desires that all sheep belong to his fold. He wants everyone in his Church.

The Good Shepherd is like the shepherd in Jesus' **parable** about the lost sheep. He pursues and saves those whose lives are in danger. In the **Old Testament**, God is depicted as a shepherd who cares for his sheep, particularly in the well-loved Psalm 23. The Good Shepherd is the most common image of Jesus in early Christian art. The Fourth Sunday of Easter is designated as Good Shepherd Sunday.

Gospel

1) The word *gospel* comes from the Old English word for "good news." The Gospel is the good news of our **Salvation** achieved through Jesus Christ. Jesus charged his followers to proclaim it to all the world.

2) The Gospels are the four written records in the Bible about God's saving action in sending Jesus. The Gospel of Matthew, written for Jewish converts, presents Jesus as the fulfillment of **Old Testament** prophecies. The Gospel of Mark, probably the first account written, is directed to **Gentile** converts (Romans). It is short and fast-paced and presents Jesus as a man of action. The Gospel of Luke was written for Gentile converts in Greece. Its main theme is salvation for all, especially the poor. It is known as the Gospel of mercy, women, prayer, the Holy Spirit, and joy.

The first three Gospels are called **Synoptic** because they are similar in their content and order of events. The Gospel of John is unique in that it focuses on Jesus' role of redeeming humanity instead of on his earthly healing and teaching. Besides being poetic and symbolic, John's Gospel is highly theological and stresses that Jesus is the Son of God.

Every Mass includes a reading from the Gospel. We stand for the reading out of respect for the Christ it presents to us. Like the priest, we make a small Sign of the Cross with our thumb on our forehead, lips, and breast. As we do so, we may pray, "Lord, may your word be in my mind, on my lips, and in my heart."

grace

Grace is a **supernatural** gift from God that enables us to live as his children.

1. Sanctifying grace is a share in the life of God and God's friendship. It is God dwelling within us. We receive this divine life at **Baptism**, and it remains in us unless we commit a **mortal sin** and turn completely against God.

2. Actual grace is a divine aid that inspires and empowers us to do something good. For example, we experience actual grace when the thought occurs to us to perform an act of charity or to say a prayer.

3. Sacramental grace is the special grace each **sacrament** provides. The Sacrament of Penance, for instance, gives us the grace to withstand **temptation**.

grace at meals

Prayers of blessing and thanksgiving before and after meals are called grace. We offer these prayers to acknowledge that our food is a gift from God. They may be spontaneous or traditional.

Gregorian chant

Gregorian chant is church music with one simple melody line. It is named for Pope Saint Gregory the Great because he called for church music to be collected and organized in the sixth century. Some chants are still used in the **liturgy** today.

guardian angels

Guardian **angels** are powerful, created spirits appointed by God to watch over us. They are also called holy watchers. Our angels are friends who help us live as God's children, pray for us, and take our prayers to Heaven. Jesus said that guardian angels always look on our Heavenly Father's face. (Matthew 18:10) Some people believe that a guardian angel watches over every parish, city, and nation. A few saints, such as Saint Frances of Rome and Saint Pio of Pietrelcina, saw and spoke with guardian angels. We celebrate the Feast of the Guardian Angels on October 2. It is good to pray the Prayer to the Guardian Angel every day.

H

habit

1) A habit is an ingrained way of doing things developed by repeated actions. A good habit is a **virtue**, and a bad habit is a **vice**.

2) The distinctive clothing worn by members of religious institutes is called a habit. It marks them as **consecrated** men and women and identifies them as members of a particular community. Habits for sisters vary from dresses and veils to rings, pins, or crosses.

Hail Mary

The Hail Mary is the most common prayer to Mary, the Mother of God. It honors her by repeating words spoken to her by the angel Gabriel at the **Annunciation** and by her cousin Elizabeth at the **Visitation**. The word *Jesus* was added to identify "the fruit of your womb." The Church added the last sentence that asks for Mary's prayers. When we pray the **Rosary**, we pray the Hail Mary 53 times. In Latin the name of this prayer is *Ave Maria*. Composers have set the Latin version of the Hail Mary to beautiful music.

halo

In religious art a halo is a thin, circular band or a solid disk of light surrounding or above a person's head to represent holiness. Halos were first added to images of Jesus and later to images of Mary, angels, and saints.

Heaven

Heaven is the place where God lives with the angels and saints. There he is seen face-to-face and enjoyed by all. Heaven is the state of perfect and eternal happiness promised to believers and what we long for. It is God's kingdom of peace, justice, and love. The degree of happiness experienced in Heaven depends on how much **grace** (friendship with God) a person has at death. At the **resurrection** at the end of time, the faithful will be taken to Heaven body and **soul**. Now only Jesus and Mary are there body and soul. People do not become **angels** (pure spirits) in Heaven, but their bodies are glorified. *Paradise* is another word for Heaven.

Hell

Hell is the opposite of **Heaven**. It is the place or state of eternal separation from God. This causes great suffering. The **angels** who rebelled against God are in Hell. People who reject God's love and mercy and die unrepentant doom themselves to this never-ending pain. They are also excluded from the company of the **saints** in Heaven. In the New Testament, Hell is associated with fire and darkness.

heresy

A heresy is a Catholic's denial of a Church dogma, which is a truth revealed by God that must be believed. The person is known as a heretic and separates himself or herself from the **Church**.

hermit

A hermit is a person who lives alone and in silence in order to contemplate or focus on God. The life of a hermit is one of **prayer**, **penance**, and the **evangelical counsels**. In the past, people sought out hermits for advice on the spiritual life. This solitary way of life began in the fourth century and evolved into monastic communities. Saint Paul of Thebes was the first Christian hermit. Today hermits are members of religious institutes or individuals consecrated by a diocesan bishop. A hermit resides in a hermitage. An example of a contemporary hermit is Sister Wendy Beckett, who became known for her books and TV show about art.

hierarchy

The hierarchy of the Church is the **pope** and the **bishops** who teach, govern, and sanctify the Church. They are ordained through the Sacrament of **Holy Orders** to carry out Church ministry. The hierarchy traces back to the **Apostles** who were chosen by Jesus with **Peter** as their leader. Their power was passed on through the imposition of hands down to the present day.

Holy Days of Obligation

Holy Days of Obligation are feasts so important that we are required to celebrate them by participating in the **Eucharist**. In the United States, there are six Holy Days of Obligation: the Solemnity of Mary, Mother of God (January 1), Ascension (forty days after Easter), Assumption of the Blessed Virgin (August 15), All Saints Day (November 1), Immaculate Conception (December 8), and Christmas (December 25). When January 1 or August 15 falls on a Saturday or Monday, there is no obligation to attend Mass.

Holy Family

The members of the Holy Family are Jesus, the Blessed Virgin Mary, and Joseph, who is the foster father of Jesus. They lived together in Nazareth in the province of Galilee. The Feast of the Holy Family is the Sunday after Christmas, or December 30 if Christmas falls on a Sunday. Devotion to the Holy Family is meaningful today when many families are struggling. A pious custom is to write the initials JMJ on papers in honor of the Holy Family.

Holy Father

Holy Father is a title for the **pope**. It signifies his role as spiritual father of the whole Church. The word *pope* comes from Latin and Greek words that mean "father."

holy hour

A holy hour is a devotion that consists of an hour of prayer before the exposed **Blessed Sacrament**. It originated with Saint Margaret Mary Alacoque in the seventeenth century. She had a vision where Jesus taught her that making holy hours would show devotion to the **Sacred Heart**. By this practice we answer Jesus' question in the garden of **Gethsemane**: "So you could not keep watch with me for one hour?" (Matthew 26:40)

Holy Land

See **Israel**.

Holy Name of Jesus

In the Gospels the angel Gabriel told Mary to name her son Jesus. In a dream an angel also told Joseph that Mary's son was to be named Jesus. The name Jesus means "God saves." A monogram for it is **IHS**. Because the name Jesus stands for the all-holy one, we treat it with respect. Some people bow their head at the name of Jesus. Just saying "Jesus" in itself is a short prayer. Jesus promised that whatever we ask the Father for in his name will be granted. That is why many of our prayers end with "in the name of Jesus."

Since the thirteenth century, the Holy Name Society has had as its main purpose to promote reverence for the name of God and the name of Jesus. Its members also perform works of mercy. The Divine Praises, which is prayed at **Benediction**, is meant to make reparation for profanity—that is, using God's name improperly.

holy oils

Holy oils are **sacramentals** used in the **sacraments**. They are blessed by the bishop on Holy Thursday and distributed to parishes. There are three kinds of oils. Holy **Chrism**, which is made from vegetable oil and balsam or perfume, is used in Baptism, Confirmation, and Holy Orders. It also is used for anointing in the dedication of churches and altars. The oil of catechumens is used in Baptism. The oil of the sick is used in the Anointing of the Sick. The holy oils are stored in containers called oil stocks. They are kept in an ambry, a cabinet that is normally in the **sanctuary**.

Holy Orders

Holy Orders is the **sacrament** in which men are ordained to receive the powers of Christ's priesthood in order to sanctify the **Church**. Jesus made the Apostles priests at the Last Supper. The Rite of Holy

Orders includes the imposition of the bishop's hands, an anointing with **Chrism**, and the bishop's prayers. There are three levels of Holy Orders: the diaconate (deacon), the presbyterate or priesthood (priest), and the episcopate (bishop). This sacrament confers a character, an indelible spiritual mark, and therefore it can be received only once.

Holy Saturday

Holy Saturday is the last day of **Holy Week** and a day of the **Holy Triduum**. It is a time for quiet reflection on the Lord in the tomb. As Bishop Melito of Sardis said long ago, "The whole earth keeps silence because the king is asleep." There is no Mass on Holy Saturday until after sundown, when the **Easter** Vigil is celebrated with much joy.

Holy See

1) The Holy See is the Church's central government, which is composed of the **pope**, the **Roman Curia**, and the diplomats to various countries. The word *see* comes from the Latin word *sedes*, which means "seat" or "chair." A seat symbolizes authority.

2) The Holy See is the residence of the pope in Rome.

holy shroud

A shroud is a burial sheet. The cloth that wrapped the body of Jesus in the tomb is called the holy shroud. In Turin, Italy, there is a cloth that many believe is the holy shroud. It bears the imprints of a crucified man. No one can explain how the imprints were made. The cloth has been tested to see how old it is, but the results were debatable.

Holy Spirit

The Holy Spirit is the Third Person of the Holy **Trinity**. The Holy Spirit is **God** and coequal and coeternal with the Father and Son. But he is distinct from them. The Holy Spirit proceeds from the Father and the Son and is described as the love between them. Although the Three Persons of the Trinity act together, the work of sanctification (making people holy) is attributed to the Holy Spirit. Jesus became man when the Holy Spirit overshadowed Mary. The Spirit was present at the baptism of Jesus in the form of a dove, which is why artists often depict the Spirit that way. At the Last Supper, Jesus promised that the Holy Spirit would be sent. This promise was fulfilled at **Pentecost** when the Holy Spirit came down on the Church and empowered the **Apostles** to witness to Jesus.

We receive the Holy Spirit and the **Gifts of the Holy Spirit** at **Baptism**. His action in us is increased at **Confirmation**. Other names for the Holy Spirit that reflect his role in the life of the Church are Counselor, **Paraclete** (Advocate), Sanctifier, and Comforter. Praying to the Holy Spirit is recommended before making a major decision, facing a challenge, reading Scripture, and fighting **temptation**.

See John 14:15–17, 25 for Jesus' promise of the Holy Spirit.

Holy Thursday

Holy Thursday is the day of **Holy Week** that marks the end of **Lent**. The **Holy Triduum** begins on Holy Thursday evening. In the morning there is usually a Chrism Mass at the cathedral. There the bishop, gathered with his priests, blesses the **holy oils** to be distributed to the parishes. Ordinarily the only Mass at parishes that day is the evening Mass of the Lord's Supper. This celebrates the institution of the Eucharist and of the priesthood. At this Mass the holy oils are received into the church. The washing of feet is carried out in imitation of Jesus who washed the Apostles' feet at the Last Supper. The Mass ends with the **Blessed Sacrament** being taken in procession to the altar of repose for adoration until midnight. The altars are stripped, and everyone leaves in silence. Holy Thursday is also called Maundy Thursday because at the Last Supper, Jesus gave a new commandment. The Latin word for command is *mandatum*.

Holy Triduum

See **Easter Triduum**.

holy water

Holy water is water that is blessed by a priest. This **sacramental** is used for Baptisms, blessing and sprinkling the congregation at Mass, and other blessings. Holy water is kept in fonts at the church doors. Some churches use the baptismal font or pool as the holy water font. We dip our fingers into holy water and bless ourselves by making the **Sign of the Cross**. This helps us recall our Baptism and renew our baptismal promises. In churches there is usually a container that dispenses holy water for home use.

Holy Week

Holy Week is the week before Easter from Passion (Palm) Sunday through Holy Saturday. During this week we pray and reflect on the Passion and Death that Jesus underwent to win **Salvation** for us. The days are filled with beautiful rituals and prayers. Eastern Churches call this week the Great Week.

holy year

The holy year, or Jubilee Year, is a year of renewal and forgiveness of sins that the pope declares usually every twenty-five years. During this year people may receive special **indulgences**. For example, those who make a **pilgrimage** to one of the four patriarchal basilicas in Rome may receive a plenary indulgence. At the opening of the holy year, the special holy doors of these **basilicas** are opened. At the end of the year, they are closed. The last Jubilee Year was 2000.

holy/holiness

1) Holiness is the quality of being free from evil. **God** is completely holy, and we are holy to the extent that we are like God. **Grace** and good deeds make us holy. Every person is called to holiness, which is

our chief goal in life. If we become holy, our destiny will be Heaven. Holiness is one of the four **Marks**, or characteristics of the Church. The work of the **Holy Spirit** is to sanctify the **Church**, that is, to make it holy.

2) People and objects are considered holy when they are consecrated to the service of God.

homily

A homily is the sermon or talk at Mass that follows the reading of the Gospel. The priest or deacon explains the Scripture readings and suggests how we can live out their message.

hope

Hope is the **Theological Virtue** that makes us desire eternal life and gives us confidence that God will provide the **grace** necessary to reach it. This virtue is given to us at **Baptism**. The symbol of hope is an anchor.

Hosanna

At every Mass we pray Hosanna as we say or sing the Holy, Holy, Holy. The word *Hosanna* expresses joy and greeting. Originally, it meant "save us." People greeted Jesus with Hosanna when he entered **Jerusalem** before his Passion. On **Passion** (Palm) Sunday, we reenact the crowd's enthusiastic welcoming of Jesus.

host

Originally, the word *host* meant a person sacrificed. Today the term refers to the bread that becomes the Body of Christ at Mass. We receive it in Holy **Communion**. The host is unleavened bread (without yeast) and looks like a wafer. The priest has a large host, which he breaks and distributes to us as a sign of unity. A large host is also reserved in the tabernacle so that it can be displayed for **exposition** and **Benediction**.

Jesus is totally present in every particle of a sacred host until it is no longer a host.

hymn

A hymn is a religious song used in worship. Jesus and the **Apostles** sang a hymn at the end of the **Last Supper** (Matthew 26:30). Saint Paul encouraged the early Christians to sing hymns (Ephesians 5:19). Saint Augustine said that singing well is praying twice. Many of today's hymns are based on psalms, songs that the Israelites sang in the Temple. A book of hymns is a hymnal.

hyperdulia (hi-per-DOO-li-a)

Hyperdulia is praise given to Mary because she is the Mother of God who played a unique role in Salvation History. It signifies a greater degree of praise than dulia, which is honor given to the angels and saints. But hyperdulia is a lesser degree of praise than is given to God, which is called latria. We praise Mary in prayers to her and through devotions such as a **May crowning**.

hypostatic union

The hypostatic union is the theological term for the union of the divine and human natures in the one divine person of Jesus. (Nature is what someone is. Person is who someone is.) God does not merely dwell in the man Jesus. Jesus is God. Saint Ephraim compared the union of natures in Jesus to the inseparable union of two colors of paint that combine to form a new color. The **doctrine** of the hypostatic union was proclaimed at the Council of Chalcedon in 451.

I

icon

An icon is a sacred image of God, Jesus, Mary, or a saint. It is usually painted on wood but may also be done in metal, in a mosaic, or embroidered. Icons are cherished and venerated by the Eastern Church as a window into Heaven. Painters of icons commonly pray and fast as they work. Colors, objects, and positions in icons have special meaning. For example, the color blue represents divinity. Three well-known icons are "The Trinity" by Andrei Rublev, "Christ Pantocrator," and "Our Lady of Perpetual Help."

idol

An idol is something that is worshiped in place of God or given more value than God. Long ago this was an animal, an object, or a person. In **Old Testament** times, people worshiped false gods like the sun and images they made from stone. Today's idols are things like money, power, or pleasure. The First **Commandment** forbids the worship of idols, which is called idolatry.

IHS

You may have seen the letters IHS in religious art. This is a monogram made from the first three letters of the Greek word for Jesus. The emblem of the Jesuits, a religious community founded by Saint Ignatius of Loyola as the Company of Jesus, is an IHS surmounted by a cross.

Immaculate Conception

The Immaculate Conception is the **dogma** that **Mary** was conceived without **Original Sin**. The purity of Mary from the first moment of her existence was a unique God-given privilege. Jesus conquered all sin by his Passion, Death, and Resurrection. The effect of his redeeming sacrifice was anticipated in his mother. It is only right that the mother of the Savior was the first one to be saved from sin. The dogma of the Immaculate Conception was declared in 1854. In 1858, the Blessed Virgin appeared to Saint Bernadette in Lourdes, France, and identified herself as the Immaculate Conception. Under this title, Mary is the patroness of the United States. The National Shrine of the Immaculate

Conception is in Washington, D.C. This **basilica** houses many shrines that represent different cultures and titles of Mary.

imprimatur

An imprimatur signifies that a religious textbook has the approval of a **bishop**. The Latin word means "let it be printed." The bishop appoints a censor to read the book to see if it is free from error regarding doctrine. If the book presents the faith correctly, the word *imprimatur* and the name of the bishop who approved the book appear on its copyright page. The name of the censor also appears after *nihil obstat*, which is Latin for "nothing prevents."

Incarnation

The Incarnation is the great mystery of God the Son becoming man in order to save us. Jesus was born of the Virgin Mary through the power of the **Holy Spirit**. A divine nature and a human nature are joined in this one person. Jesus is truly God and truly man and will always be so. We celebrate the Incarnation on March 25, and nine months later, on December 25, we celebrate the birth of Jesus.

incense

Incense is resin from trees in the form of grains or powder. When it is sprinkled on hot coals in a thurible (a censer), fragrant smoke forms. This "holy smoke" symbolizes our prayers rising to Heaven. The censer is usually swung on a chain. Incense may be used at Mass to honor the **altar**, the **Book of the Gospels**, the gifts brought up, and the congregation. At the end of a funeral Mass, the coffin is incensed to honor the deceased person in whom God lived and as a sign of our prayers for him or her. The vessel that holds the incense is called a boat because of its shape. Some people like to burn incense while they pray.

indulgence

All **sins**, even after they are forgiven, deserve punishment on earth or in **Purgatory**. An indulgence is the canceling of this punishment through certain good works and prayers. Indulgences draw on the treasury of merits of Jesus and the saints. A plenary indulgence cancels all punishment. It requires freedom from **venial sin**, confession, Holy Communion, and prayers for the pope's intentions. A partial indulgence cancels part of the punishment. It requires **contrition**. The Church determines which practices and prayers can result in an indulgence. Indulgences may be applied to oneself or to souls in **Purgatory**. Indulgences are possible because of the **Communion of Saints**, the unity among all church members. In the past, this practice was abused by people who sold indulgences, a factor that led to the Protestant Reformation.

infallibility

Infallibility is the quality of being free from error. The Church is infallible when it teaches what is in Divine **Revelation**. The pope is infallible when he speaks as pastor of the whole Church about faith or morals clearly intending that the **doctrine** be held by the entire Church. The bishops as a college or in a council are infallible when they are in communion with the pope and speak about faith or morals for the universal (entire) Church. Infallibility is due to the assistance of the **Holy Spirit**, who guides the Church.

Infancy Narratives

The Infancy Narratives are the stories about Jesus' birth and early life that are found in the **Gospels** of Luke and Matthew. We don't know how much is historical and how much is symbolic. We do know that the Infancy Narratives are inspired and reveal truths about Jesus, in particular that he is the Son of God and the **Messiah**.

Inquisition

The Inquisition was a church court that began in France in the twelfth century for the purpose of eliminating **heresy**. It existed until the early fourteenth century. The Dominican Order was given the responsibility of carrying out the inquisitions. In time, heretics who would not reform were handed over to civil authorities for punishment. In those days, heresy was equivalent to anarchy and treason, and the penalty was sometimes death.

INRI

On **crucifixes** the letters INRI often appear on a plaque above the body of Jesus. The letters are the initials of the Latin words for "Jesus of Nazareth, King of the Jews." Pontius Pilate had these words written in Hebrew, Latin, and Greek and placed above the head of Jesus on the cross. In the Roman Empire, the crime for which people were crucified was posted above them. Jesus' crime in the eyes of the Romans was claiming to be a king when Caesar was the king. They didn't know that Jesus was actually the king of the universe, and so the plaque declared the truth.

inspiration

Inspiration is the Holy Spirit's guidance in the writing of Scripture. God moved the human authors of the sacred books to write what he wanted in the way he wished. Because of inspiration, God is the author of the **Bible**, and we call it the Word of God.

intercession

An intercession is a prayer for other people. Jesus, Mary, and the saints intercede for us. We intercede for people on earth, and they intercede for us. We also intercede for the people in **Purgatory**. During the **Eucharist** most of the prayers in the Universal Prayer, or Prayer of the Faithful, are prayers of intercession.

Israel

1) Israel was the name that God gave to Jacob, the grandson of **Abraham**. Jacob's twelve sons were the fathers of twelve tribes. All the descendants of Jacob were called Israel or Israelites.

2) In the promised land of Canaan, the kingdom of the ten northern tribes was called Israel, while the two tribes of the southern kingdom were called Judah.

3) Today Israel is the country in the Middle East formed by the United Nations in 1948. It is also called the Holy Land because Jesus, the Savior of the world, was born there. In the Holy Land, large churches mark the sites where key events in the life of Jesus took place. "Jesus boats" sail the Sea of Galilee, pilgrims are baptized in the Jordan River, and people walk the Way of the Cross. The Holy Land is sometimes referred to as the fifth Gospel.

J

Jerusalem

Jerusalem was an ancient city in Palestine that was the capital of King **David**'s kingdom. After he captured the city from the Jebusites, it became known as the City of David. For the Jews, Jerusalem was the Holy City because it was where David brought the **Ark** of the Covenant and later where the Temple, the Lord's dwelling place, was built. For Christians, Jerusalem is the Holy City because it is the site of Jesus' Death and Resurrection. The Church officially began in Jerusalem on **Pentecost**, and the first Church council was held there. Saint James was the first **bishop** of Jerusalem.

Jesse tree

Jesse was the father of King **David** and an ancestor of **Jesus**. Originally, a Jesse tree was the family tree of Jesus in pictures. It depicted his genealogy. Today the concept of a Jesse tree is broader, for it holds symbols representing other major people in Salvation History. For example, a rainbow stands for Noah and a burning bush stands for **Moses**. Making a Jesse tree is an **Advent** custom. It can be drawn on paper or made by hanging symbols on a tree or tree branch set in plaster of Paris.

Jesus

Jesus is the God-Man who saved the world from **sin** and its consequences by his Passion, Death, and **Resurrection**. His holy name means "God saves." Jesus, the Son of God, was the promised **Messiah**. Through the power of the **Holy Spirit**, a Jewish virgin named Mary conceived Jesus. This mystery of God becoming man is called the **Incarnation**. Jesus lived in Nazareth of Galilee with Mary and her husband, Joseph. When he was about thirty years old, Jesus left home and began to preach about the **Kingdom of God**. He promised eternal life to those who believed in him. Jesus was also known as a healer. Not only did he cure physical ailments, but he forgave sins. He reached out to women and children, who were considered unimportant, and to people who were outcasts.

Religious authorities resented Jesus because he did not strictly follow their rules and because he made himself equal to God. Their antagonism led to the Romans sentencing Jesus to death on a **cross**. Before he was captured, Jesus ate a Last Supper with his Apostles. During it, he instituted the **Eucharist** as a memento of his death and as a way that he would be with us. Three days after his Crucifixion, Jesus rose with a new, glorified body. Then he ascended to Heaven where he lives in glory with the Father. We believe that Jesus will return at the end of the world and judge humankind. The followers of Jesus became the Christian Church led by the Apostles, men he had prepared for leadership. Jesus is the invisible head of the Church. The Bible contains four accounts of the life of Jesus called **Gospels**.

See Philippians 2:5–11, a hymn that summarizes who Jesus is.

Jesus prayer

The Jesus **prayer** is "Lord Jesus Christ, Son of God, have mercy on me, a sinner." It is repeated over and over and puts us in the presence of Jesus. This prayer probably goes back to the desert fathers of the fifth century. It combines the cry of the blind man sitting at the side of the road—"Jesus, Son of David, have pity on me!" (Luke 18:38) and the prayer of the publican in Jesus' parable—"O God, be merciful to me a sinner" (Luke 18:13). Another name for the Jesus prayer is the prayer of the heart. Some people pray it by inhaling on the first half of the Jesus prayer and exhaling on the second half.

John the Baptist

John the Baptist was the last of the Old Testament **prophets**. He is the precursor, or forerunner, of Jesus. John's mission was to prepare the world for Jesus, the **Messiah**. An **angel** announced John's birth to his father, Zechariah. Because Zechariah's wife, Elizabeth, was too old to have children, he doubted the angel. For that, he lost the power of speech. The angel directed Zechariah to name his son John. Mary, the mother of Jesus and a cousin of Elizabeth, came to help Elizabeth during her pregnancy. When Mary arrived, Elizabeth told her that the child leapt in her womb. After the baby was born, people discussed what to call him. Zechariah wrote that his name was to be John, and he regained his voice.

When John grew up, he lived in the desert clad in camel hair clothing and living on locusts. He called people to repent and be baptized in the Jordan River as a sign of their repentance. John baptized Jesus and identified him as the Lamb of God to two of his followers. For criticizing King Herod's unlawful marriage, John was imprisoned. At a royal banquet, the daughter of Herod's wife danced. Herod foolishly promised the girl anything she wanted. At her mother's prodding, she asked for John's head on a platter. So John was beheaded. Jesus once praised John as the greatest man ever born of a woman (Luke 7:28).

We celebrate two feasts in Saint John the Baptist's honor: his birth on June 24 and his death on August 29.

See Matthew 3:1–12 for John the Baptist's messages.

Joseph

Joseph is the legal father of Jesus and the husband of Mary. As such, he is the head of the Holy Family. Joseph, who was known as a just or righteous man, is the highest-ranking saint after Mary. He was a carpenter or construction worker in Nazareth and taught Jesus not only his trade but how to be a Jewish man.

While betrothed to Mary, Joseph learned that she was pregnant. He kindly decided to divorce her quietly. But then an angel appeared to Joseph in a dream and told him that Mary's child was conceived by the power of the Holy Spirit. Her son was going to be the Savior, and Joseph was to name him Jesus. When Joseph had to go to Bethlehem for the census, Mary went with him. There Jesus was born. In another dream, an angel told Joseph to flee to Egypt because King Herod was seeking to destroy Jesus. After Herod died, an angel directed Joseph to return to Israel. The Holy Family moved to Nazareth in Galilee. When Jesus was twelve, his family went to Jerusalem for the Passover, and Mary and Joseph lost him for three anxious days. The Gospel doesn't mention Joseph after that, so we assume that he died before Jesus left Nazareth to teach. If so, Mary and Jesus were probably with him at his death. For that reason Joseph is the patron of a happy death. He is also the patron of workers and of the universal Church, which is the Body of Christ. We celebrate the feast of Saint Joseph on March 19 and the feast of Saint Joseph the Worker on May 1. Joseph's name is mentioned in every Eucharistic Prayer.

St. Joseph Oratory in Montreal, Quebec, Canada, is the largest church in honor of Saint Joseph. The humble **brother** Saint André Bessette, C.S.C., was the force behind its construction. Some people pray to Saint Joseph when they are trying to sell their home. They bury a statue of him on the property and pray to him. When the house sells, they display the statue of Joseph in their new home.

Jubilee Year

See **holy year.**

Judah/Judea

Judah was the southern region of Palestine and home to the tribes of Judah and Benjamin. **Jerusalem** was its capital city, where the Temple, the center of Jewish religion, was located. Judea is the Greek and Roman translation of Judah. The word *Jew* comes from Judea.

judgment

All people can expect to be judged twice. At the moment of death, they will know if their lives deserve punishment in **Hell**, happiness in **Heaven**, or purification in **Purgatory**. This is called the particular judgment. At the end of time when Christ returns, he will judge all people. Their eternal destiny will be revealed. This is known as the general or Last Judgment. Saint John of the Cross said that in the end everyone will be judged on **love.**

Justification

Justification is the process of becoming right with God, or holy. Sinners are justified by **faith** in Christ and good works. By being justified, we give honor to God and become heirs of **Heaven.**

K

kerygma (keh-RIHG-muh)

Kerygma is the message of the Good News of **Salvation** that the **disciples** of Jesus proclaim to the world. This Greek word means "preaching."

Kingdom of God

The Kingdom of God is the reign of God over the universe. It is a kingdom of justice, peace, and love. God's kingdom is here but not yet. It is here to the extent that God's will is done, and it is present but undeveloped in the **Church**. But God's kingdom is not here yet because its fullness will be at the end of the world in Heaven, where it will be everlasting. Each time we pray the **Lord's Prayer**, we ask that God's kingdom may come. Jesus gave us the **Beatitudes**, which describe the people who belong to the kingdom. He also told several **parables** about the Kingdom of God, sometimes comparing it to a banquet.

See Matthew 13:44–52; 25:1–13 and Mark 4:26–32 for parables about the kingdom.

Knights of Columbus

The Knights of Columbus is a society for Catholic laymen. It is named for Christopher Columbus. Founded in Connecticut in 1882 by the priest Venerable Michael J. McGivney, the Knights of Columbus spread to other countries. Now there are almost two million members. The Knights serve the Church in many ways and donate large sums to charity. The organization provides insurance for its members. At church events and in parades, you might see the Knights in their colorful garb that features naval hats and swords. The women's counterpart organization is the Daughters of Isabella.

L

labyrinth

Retreat centers and churches are popularizing an old method of prayer by having a labyrinth carved into greenery or painted on canvas. During the Middle Ages, Christians often made a **pilgrimage** to Jerusalem. Those who couldn't make that holy journey walked a labyrinth at one of seven European cathedrals. The labyrinth in the floor of the cathedral in Chartres, France, is the only one remaining. A labyrinth is not a maze, which has many paths and is meant to confuse. The labyrinth, usually circular, has one path that leads from the outside through winding turns to the center (the New Jerusalem, or God) and back again to the world. The path is like the journey of life. It can be walked with a Scripture verse in mind, a feeling, a question, or simply noticing thoughts and feelings. A labyrinth on paper or on the Internet can be "walked" with your fingers.

laity/laypeople

The laity is all the men and women in the Church who are not members of the **clergy**. This includes men and women religious who are not ordained. Through their **Baptism** the laity shares in three roles of **Christ**. They are priestly because they offer Jesus and themselves at the Eucharist. They are **prophets** because they proclaim the Gospel to the world. And they are royal because they are heirs to the Kingdom of God. All members of the laity are called to **holiness**. They are to bring about the sanctification of the world.

last sacraments

The last **sacraments** are Penance, Anointing of the Sick, and viaticum (Holy Communion) when they are administered to a person who is dying. Confirmation may be included if the person hasn't celebrated it. These final sacraments prepare people for the next life and their meeting with God by forgiving their sins and filling them with grace, which is divine life. When someone is dying, it is good to call a priest so that the person receives the comfort of these sacraments that Jesus provides.

Last Supper

The Last Supper is the meal that Jesus ate with his Apostles in Jerusalem on the night before he died. This supper may have been a

Passover meal, which Jews eat each year in memory of God's saving them from slavery in Egypt. At this supper, Jesus instituted the Eucharist as a memorial of his Passion and Death. Jesus declared that the bread was his body and the wine was his blood. He offered himself as a **sacrifice** to the Father, and he gave the gift of priesthood to the **Apostles**. Jesus told them, "Do this in remembrance of me." At that meal Jesus washed the feet of the Apostles as a lesson that they were to be servants of the Church. At each Mass the priest repeats the words that Jesus said in instituting the **Eucharist** and offers the same sacrifice.

latria (LAH-tree-ah)

Latria is the unique **adoration** or praise that we give to God as the Supreme Being and our Creator. Our greatest act of adoration is the **Eucharist**. Latria is different from the honor we give to Mary, which is called hyperdulia, and to the saints, which is called dulia.

lectio divina (LEHK-see-oh duh-VEE-nah)

Lectio divina is Latin for "sacred reading." It is a method of **prayer** that has four steps:

1. Read a passage, usually from the Bible.
2. When a word or phrase attracts your attention, stop and reflect on why it is important to you. What is God saying to you in it?
3. When you realize the meaning of the word or phrase for you, respond in prayer. This could be a prayer of praise, thanksgiving, contrition, petition, or **intercession**.
4. Be quiet and rest in the presence of God. The goal of *lectio divina* is this final step, which is **contemplation**, the highest form of prayer.

Lectionary

A *Lectionary* is the official book of **Scripture** readings for the Mass. The readings for the Sunday Mass are in three cycles: A, B, and C.

Sunday readings include two passages from the Old Testament or New Testament, a psalm, a Gospel acclamation, and a Gospel reading. A new cycle begins with Advent. The weekday readings are on a two-year cycle, year 1 and year 2. They have only one Scripture reading other than the Gospel. The person who proclaims the First or Second Readings is called a **lector**. The **Book of the Gospels** is a book from which the Gospel readings are read.

lector

A lector is a person who reads the First or Second Readings. Proclaiming God's Word for the community is an important ministry.

Lent

Lent is the season of the **liturgical year** that prepares us to celebrate **Easter**. It is forty days of penance that begin with Ash Wednesday and end on Holy Thursday. The number forty stands for the forty days of prayer and fasting that Jesus spent in the desert. During Lent we fast, pray, give alms, and perform acts of **penance**. We make resolutions in order to eliminate our faults and practice self-control. The priest wears violet vestments at Mass, and the joyful word *Alleluia* is not said. The **Stations of the Cross** are commonly prayed during Lent. On Fridays in Lent, we do not eat meat. A good Lent leads to a happy Easter.

litany

A litany is a prayer that addresses God or a saint by many titles. After each title is said, a response is repeated. Common litanies are the Litany of Loreto, the Litany of the Sacred Heart, and the Litany of Divine Mercy. A litany usually begins by addressing the **Trinity** and ends with invocations to the Lamb of God.

liturgical colors

See **colors, liturgical**.

liturgical year

Our regular year begins January 1, but the Church has its own year, which begins on the First Sunday of **Advent**. Also called the Church year, the liturgical year is the annual cycle during which the Church celebrates the mysteries of Christ and honors Mary, the angels, and the saints. These mysteries and people are celebrated in the Mass, the **Liturgy of the Hours**, and other acts of worship. The liturgical year revolves around the **Incarnation** (during Advent and Christmas) and the **redemption** (during Lent and Easter). In between we celebrate Ordinary Time, whose weeks are referred to by ordinal numbers. The Feast of Christ the King is the last Sunday of the liturgical year.

liturgy

The liturgy is the Church's public worship of God that expresses who we are as God's people. Through the liturgy, Christ continues his work of **redemption**. The foremost liturgies are the seven **sacraments**, especially the **Eucharist**, and the **Liturgy of the Hours**. But liturgy includes **Benediction**, **rites** for men and women religious, blessings, and funeral rites. The liturgy is celebrated by the people of God and conducted by a priest or deacon. It involves words, symbols, and actions. Its rites are approved by the Holy See and found in official books. Private devotions such as the **Rosary** are not liturgy.

Liturgy of the Hours

The Liturgy of the Hours, formerly called the Divine Office, is the official daily prayer of the Church. It is meant to be the prayer of all Christians. The Liturgy of the Hours makes the entire day holy. Priests pray certain hours from their prayer book called a breviary. Most men and women religious pray a few of the hours. Contemplative communities, who never leave their house, pray the full cycle, rising during the night to do so.

The Liturgy of the Hours includes the following prayers (their former Latin names in parentheses). The two main prayers, which are sometimes prayed in parishes, are Morning Prayer (Lauds) and Evening Prayer (Vespers). These are called the hinge prayers of the cycle. There are three brief Midday Prayers: Midmorning (Terce), Midday (Sext), and Midafternoon (None). The last prayer of the day is Night Prayer (Compline). An Office of Readings contains psalms and passages from Scripture and the **Fathers of the Church**. The chief hours include **psalms**, a **canticle**, intercessions, and the **Lord's Prayer**. The Benedictus is prayed in Morning Prayer, the Magnificat is prayed in Evening Prayer, and the Nunc Dimittus is prayed in Night Prayer. The prayers of the Liturgy of the Hours correspond to the seasons and feast days of the **liturgical year**.

Lord

Lord is the title that stands for the holy name of God. It is a substitute for God's personal name, Yahweh. The Jews showed reverence for God by not saying or writing his personal name. Jesus is called Lord. This means that he is God and has supreme authority and power. Jesus is king over Heaven and earth. He showed his lordship in the **miracles** he worked and by triumphing over sin and death. We call him Lord Jesus or Our Lord. The Bible ends with the prayer "Come, Lord Jesus!"

Lord's Prayer

Jesus gave us the Lord's Prayer, or the Our Father, when the **Apostles** asked him to teach them how to pray. It is the model for all prayer. The early Christians prayed the Lord's Prayer three times a day. We pray it at Mass, and the Church hands it to **catechumens** in a special rite.

The Lord's Prayer has seven petitions. We ask that God's name be regarded as holy. We pray that his kingdom of peace, justice, and love may soon appear on earth with the second coming of Jesus. Then we pray that God's will, which always brings about good, may be done on earth. We ask for our daily bread: what we need to live and in particular the bread of the Eucharist. We ask God to forgive us to the extent that we forgive people who have hurt us. We also ask God to keep us from yielding to temptation. Finally, we ask to be delivered from Satan and all the evils he causes.

Other Christians add a **doxology** to the Lord's Prayer that was prayed by the early Church. At our Eucharist we pray this doxology after a priest prays a short prayer after the Lord's Prayer.

In the *Catechism of the Catholic Church*, the fourth and last book, which is about prayer, has a thorough explanation of the Lord's Prayer.

love

See **charity**.

Lucifer

Lucifer is the name that the **Fathers of the Church** gave to Satan, the leader of the fallen angels. It means "light bearer." Although Satan was once an angel of light, he now is the Prince of Darkness.

M

Madonna

Madonna is a title of the Blessed Virgin Mary that means "my lady" in Italian. Usually Mary is called "the Madonna." The term specifically refers to Mary as she appears in art with or without the infant Jesus. Some examples are Madonna of the Cherries, Madonna of the Rocks, and Madonna of the Street.

Magi

You probably are familiar with the Christmas carol "We Three Kings." These kings were really Magi, wise men, perhaps astrologers, from the East. Matthew 2:1–18 tells of these Gentiles who followed the star to the newborn king and foiled King Herod's attempt to destroy him.

Tradition holds that there were three Magi because of their three gifts of gold, frankincense, and myrrh. It is said that their names were Caspar, Melchior, and Balthazar. There could have been more, however. We celebrate the visit of the Magi on **Epiphany**.

Magisterium

The Magisterium is the teaching authority of the **Church**. It is invested in the **pope** and the college of **bishops**. They teach the faith taught by Christ and handed down through the **Apostles**. They interpret Revelation for us as presented in **Scripture** and **Tradition**.

mantra

A mantra is a word or phrase that is repeated as a **prayer**. For example, "The Lord is my shepherd" becomes a mantra when it is said over and over. Praying a mantra is a good way to pray when you are too tired, sick, or worried to pray any other way. This rhythmic method of prayer is not only comforting, but it makes you aware of God's loving presence. Mantras can also be sung.

Marks of the Church

The Marks of the **Church** are four qualities by which the Church is identified as the true Church. They are one, holy, catholic, and apostolic. The Church is one in that the members believe the same **doctrines**, celebrate the same **sacraments**, and are united under the **pope**. The Church is holy in Jesus, the founder; the sacraments; and the members. The Church is catholic, which means universal or for all people. The Church is apostolic, which means teaching what Jesus taught as handed on by the **Apostles**. The Church is also apostolic because the leaders, the pope and bishops, trace their authority back to the Apostles. We name the marks whenever we pray the **Nicene Creed** at Mass.

marriage

See **Matrimony**.

martyr

A martyr is a person who is put to death for the **faith**. The word means "witness." A martyr witnesses to faith in Jesus despite facing suffering and death. All martyrs are **saints** although they haven't all been canonized. It is said that the blood of martyrs is the seed of Christians. The brave witness of the martyrs persuades others to believe. The early Church endured and grew under Roman persecutions. Saint Stephen, a **deacon**, was the first martyr.

See Acts of the Apostles 6:1—7:60 for the story of Saint Stephen.

Mary

Mary is the Mother of God, the Queen of Heaven and Earth, and our Blessed Mother. She was a young girl in Nazareth betrothed to a carpenter named **Joseph** when the **angel** Gabriel appeared to her. God sent Gabriel to announce his plan of Salvation. Mary was chosen to bear Jesus, the Savior of the world. She agreed, calling herself God's handmaid. That day the virgin Mary conceived Jesus through the power of the **Holy Spirit**. The angel also told Mary that her elderly cousin Elizabeth was pregnant. Mary made the long journey to help Elizabeth. The older woman recognized that Mary was the mother of the Savior. On that occasion Mary praised God in the **canticle** the Magnificat.

While Mary and Joseph were in Bethlehem for a census, she gave birth to Jesus in a shelter for animals. Shepherds came and adored him. On the day that Jesus was presented in the Temple, a prophet named Simeon greeted him as the **Messiah**. Simeon predicted much sorrow for Mary. His predictions came true, and therefore we call Mary the Sorrowful Mother. When King Herod sought to kill the child Jesus, the Holy Family fled to Egypt. After Herod died, they moved to

Nazareth. When Jesus was twelve, the family went to Jerusalem for the Passover, and Jesus was lost for three days. His parents discovered him talking with teachers in the Temple, which he called his Father's house. Mary pondered this mystery.

Jesus worked his first **miracle** at Mary's prompting. At a wedding in Cana, the wine ran out. When Mary pointed out the need, Jesus turned water into wine. This event points to Mary's role of intercessor today. She prays to God for us. During the Crucifixion, Mary stood at the foot of the cross. As he was dying, Jesus entrusted her to John the Apostle. She is our mother because she cooperated in the redemption that gave us new life. Saint John Vianney said that "the love of all mothers put together is but as ice in comparison" to the love Mary has for us. After Jesus rose, Mary was with the Apostles on Pentecost when the Holy Spirit came down upon them.

We don't know if Mary died, but at the end of her life God took her, body and soul, to Heaven. Now she is known as the greatest saint and Queen of Heaven and Earth. The mystery of the **Assumption** is one of the privileges that Mary enjoyed because she is the Mother of God. She was also free from sin from the moment of her existence (the Immaculate Conception). Another privilege is that she was always a virgin even though she was the mother of Jesus.

Our Blessed Mother has appeared several times, asking us to pray and do penance. Her most famous appearances were to Saint Bernadette at Lourdes, France; to three children at Fatima, Portugal; and to Saint Juan Diego in Mexico City. Some of her many titles stem from these appearances. For example, Our Lady of Guadalupe is based on her appearance to Juan Diego. Under this title she is the patroness of the Americas. Other titles of Mary come from paintings of her, for example, Our Lady of Perpetual Help. At the **Vatican Council II**, Mary was given the title Mother of the Church. We address Mary by many of her titles when we pray the Litany of Loreto. The **Rosary**, the **scapular**, the **Miraculous Medal**, and **May crowning** are devotions to Mary.

Mary Magdalene

Saint Mary Magdalene was one of the women **disciples** who journeyed with Jesus and the **Apostles** and helped support them. She probably came from the town of Magdala in Galilee. Mary has been incorrectly identified as Mary of Bethany and the sinful woman. The only information the Gospels offer about Mary Magdalene's background is that Jesus cured her of seven **devils**. In her culture, this probably meant that Jesus cured her of a serious illness. However, the reference to devils and the identification with the sinful woman led people to regard Mary as a repentant sinner.

Mary is one of the few people named who faithfully and courageously stood near the **cross**. In the Gospel of John, on Easter morning, Mary was the first to go to Jesus' tomb. When she found that the stone at the entrance had been moved, she ran to tell Peter and the beloved disciple. After these two disciples looked at the tomb and left, Mary remained, weeping. Jesus appeared to her and asked why she was crying. Mistaking him for the gardener, she told him that if he had removed the body, he should tell her and she would take it away. But then Jesus spoke her name, and Mary recognized him. He cautioned her not to hold on to him. Jesus sent Mary to tell the disciples that he lived. She announced to them, "I have seen the Lord." Because she was sent to relay this Good News, Mary is called the Apostle to the Apostles. We celebrate her feast day on July 22.

See John 20:1–18 for the story of Mary Magdalene and the risen Lord.

Mass

See **Eucharist**.

Matrimony

Marriage is the **sacrament** that unites a man and a woman in love. Their mutual consent to give themselves to each other is not only a contract but a **covenant**. They **vow** to love each other exclusively and forever. The goal of marriage is twofold: the good of the spouses and the procreation and education of children. Marriage is also called the Sacrament of Matrimony. The **graces** that accompany the sacrament help the couple live out their **vocation**. Married love is an image of the strong, faithful love of Christ for his Church.

See John 2:1–11 for the story of Jesus celebrating a wedding at Cana.

May crowning

Since the sixteenth century, Catholics have been honoring **Mary** during the month of May. One devotion carried out in this month is a May crowning in which an image of Mary is crowned. A procession and hymns are part of this prayer service in honor of Mary, Queen of Heaven and Earth.

medal

In addition to wearing crosses, Catholics wear medals. A religious medal is a small piece of metal or plastic that is imprinted with an image of Jesus, Mary, or a saint and perhaps a short prayer. A medal is worn around the neck or pinned on clothing as a sign of devotion. A blessed medal is a **sacramental**. Popular medals are the **Miraculous Medal**, a **scapular** medal, and a Saint Christopher medal.

mediator

When two parties are at odds, another person might help resolve the problem. This person who acts as a go-between is a mediator. **Jesus** is the one great mediator between God and us. His life and Death reconciled us to God. Mary is called the mediator of grace for two reasons.

She gave birth to the Savior, and through her intercession we obtain grace from God.

meditation

Meditation is a form of mental **prayer** in which we think about God and the truths of the faith. We focus on a passage from the Bible or a religious truth and ponder its meaning. The aims of meditation are an increased knowledge of Christ, a deeper love of God, and a stronger union with him. Meditation is a step in *lectio divina* and a component of the **Rosary**. Saint Ignatius taught a form of meditation that involves imagining that you are taking part in a biblical scene. Saint Francis de Sales taught that meditation should lead to a resolution. Saint Pio of Pietrelcina said, "Through the study of books one seeks God; by meditation one finds him."

Memorare

The *Memorare* is a popular prayer asking for Mary's intercession. Its name is Latin for its first word, "remember." This prayer has been known at least since the fifteenth century.

mental prayer

When you hear the word *prayer*, you probably first think of prayers that we recite out loud. Mental prayer is an internal form of prayer, not vocalized. Speaking to God silently, **meditation**, and **contemplation** (enjoying God's presence) are forms of mental prayer. Blessed Teresa of Calcutta said that holiness is impossible without mental prayer.

Messiah

The Messiah is the one God promised to send. The Jews expected a king or **prophet** who would save them from their enemies, like Rome, which oppressed them in the time of Jesus. The Messiah would bring peace and happiness. Jesus was the true Messiah who accomplished more than what was expected. He delivered all people from sin and death. *Messiah* is the Hebrew word for "anointed one." The Greek word for Messiah is *Christos*.

metanoia (met-a-NOY-a)

Metanoia is a Greek word that means a change of heart, or a conversion. It has to do with turning away from sin through **repentance** and **penance**. John the Baptist, Jesus, and the Apostles called for a *metanoia* as a condition for entering the **Kingdom of God**.

ministry

Ministry is serving God by serving others. The term originally referred to an official role during the celebration of the **Eucharist** or other **sacraments**. Today in common usage it refers to any way that a person serves the people of God as a means to live the faith. For example, a parish might have a ministry of consolation to attend funeral Masses, a ministry of prayer to pray for parishioners in need, or a music ministry to provide music for liturgies.

miracle

A miracle is an event that does not follow any laws of nature and can only be attributed to God. Miracles are also called wonders or signs. Miracles reveal truths. For example, in the **Old Testament** the parting of the Red Sea that allowed the Israelites to escape slavery was a sign of God's saving love. The many cures that Jesus worked show his power over evil. God sometimes works miracles through saints. Once there was only enough flour to make three loaves of bread at an orphanage. Saint John Vianney told the bakers to use what they had, and the dough multiplied. In the process of **canonization**, miracles through a candidate's intercession are required as proof that the person is a saint. But we can't always expect miracles. Saint Ignatius of Loyola is said to have advised, "Pray as though everything depended on God, but work as though everything depended on you."

Miraculous Medal

The Miraculous Medal is a **sacramental** that the Blessed Virgin instructed Saint Catherine Labouré to have made in 1830. When Catherine was a young sister in the Daughters of Charity in Paris, **Mary** appeared to her three times. During one appearance, Catherine had a vision of the medal. The front shows Mary standing on the world and crushing the serpent's head. Rays stream from her hands to the world just as the graces she obtains for us do. A prayer is inscribed along the edge: "O Mary, conceived without sin, pray for us who have recourse to thee." Twenty-four years later the **dogma** of the Immaculate Conception was proclaimed. On the back of the medal is the letter *M* for Mary surmounted by the cross. Below this symbol are the Sacred Heart of Jesus circled with thorns and the Sacred Heart of Mary pierced with a sword. At the top of both hearts are flames that represent their love for us. Around the edge of the medal are twelve stars based on the vision of Mary in Revelation 12:1. Mary promised great graces to those who wear the medal. Because of the many miracles obtained by those who wore this medal, it became known as the Miraculous Medal.

missal/missalette

A missal contains the prayers and readings for the celebration of the **Eucharist** throughout the year. A short form of a missal for a congregation is called a missalette. This is a seasonal publication that includes the Sunday readings and hymns. The *Roman Missal* contains the prayers and directives for the Latin Rite of the Mass. So does a Sacramentary.

mission

1) The word *mission* comes from the Latin word for "sent." A mission is something that a person is sent to do. Jesus sent the Church to

continue his mission, namely to proclaim the Gospel and make **disciples** of all nations.

2) A mission is a religious presence within a country for the purpose of spreading the Good News where it hasn't been heard. It can also refer to the church or the territory where this takes place.

3) A parish mission is a few days when people gather to pray and listen to a speaker for the purpose of renewing their spiritual life.

missionary

A missionary is a person who spreads the faith among people who have not heard it. Missionaries usually help people meet their basic needs, such as food, clothing, housing, and good health. A foreign missionary works in a country that is not his or her own. A home missionary works in his or her native land. Another name for missionary is missioner. Some religious communities were founded to be missionary orders. One example is the Maryknoll Missioners founded in the United States in 1911. A number of saints were missionaries, such as Saint Francis Xavier, Saint Isaac Jogues, Saint Frances Xavier Cabrini, and Saint Marianne Cope.

miter

A miter is the tall, usually pointed hat that a **bishop** or **abbot** wears during liturgical celebrations. Supposedly the miter's shape represents the flames that came down upon the Apostles at Pentecost. Two bands of material called lappets hang down the back.

monastery

A monastery is the home of a religious community of **monks** or **nuns** who pray the **Liturgy of the Hours** together. Some of these communities are contemplative, solely devoted to prayer. Others may engage in **ministries** in the world.

monk

A monk is a man who belongs to a religious community that is led by an abbot. Monks live together in a monastery, take vows, and follow a specific rule of life. They pray the **Liturgy of the Hours** together and usually wear **habits**. Monks may be lay **brothers**, deacons, or priests. Saint Benedict founded Western monasticism in the sixth century.

monotheism

Monotheism is belief in one, personal **God**. Judaism, Christianity, and Islam are monotheistic religions. Belief in many gods is polytheism.

monsignor

Monsignor is an honorary title that may be given to a priest because of his important position or his years of faithful service. All **bishops** and archbishops may have this title. The word comes from the Italian for "my Lord." A priest becomes a monsignor when his bishop submits his name to the pope, and the pope declares him a monsignor. A monsignor may wear a **cassock** with red or fuschia buttons or piping. He is considered a member of the papal household.

monstrance

A monstrance is the sacred vessel used to display the **Blessed Sacrament** for **exposition** or **Benediction**. The word comes from the Latin word for "show." The sacred host is placed in a round glass enclosure called a luna, which is inserted into the monstrance. Monstrances are usually made of precious metal and decorated with rays coming forth from the window. They have a stem, which the priest holds when raising the Blessed Sacrament for a **blessing** during Benediction.

morality

Morality is the rightness or wrongness of an action or desire. The basic moral law is to do good and avoid evil. The morality of a deed depends on the person's intention, how serious the deed is, and the circumstances. The **Ten Commandments** is the moral code found in the Bible. Jesus gave us the Great Commandment to love as he does.

Morning Offering

The Morning Offering is a prayer in which we dedicate everything we do during the day to God. Saint John Vianney said that all that we do is wasted without offering it to God. The *Catechism of the Catholic Church* notes that Christians begin each day with the **Sign of the Cross**. There are several forms of the Morning Offering. The most common is the one promoted by the Apostleship of Prayer. In it we pray for the pope's intentions. Every year the pope presents a general intention and a missionary intention for each month. Of course, you can add your own intentions.

mortal sin

A mortal wound is a deadly wound. Likewise, a mortal sin is a deadly **sin**. It is a very serious sin, such as murder, that totally robs a person of a divine life of grace. This prevents him or her from entering Heaven. Three conditions determine a mortal sin: it must be a serious matter, there must be reflection on the sin, and there must be full consent. Other factors may come into play to make the sinner less guilty, such as immaturity. A mortal sin can be forgiven in the Sacrament of **Penance**. A person who commits a mortal sin may not receive Holy Communion until the sin is forgiven.

Moses

Did you ever hear someone exclaim, "Holy Moses"? Moses is the great Jewish **prophet** who led the Israelites out of slavery in Egypt. When the Pharaoh decreed that all male Jewish babies be killed, the mother of Moses hid him in a basket. The Pharaoh's daughter found Moses and raised him. After Moses killed an Egyptian, he fled to Midian. God spoke to Moses through a burning bush and told Moses to tell the Pharaoh to let his people go. After a series of ten plagues, the

Pharaoh was finally persuaded to release the Israelites. On the night of the tenth plague, the oldest son in each family died. Following God's instructions, the Israelites applied the blood of a lamb to their lintels and doorposts to protect them from this plague. They ate a meal of lamb and then left. When the Egyptians pursued them, God empowered Moses to part the Red Sea so that the Israelites escaped along a dry path.

During the forty-year journey through the desert, Moses led the people and interceded with God for them. He instructed them how to gather manna to eat, and he provided water from a rock. Through Moses, God also gave his people the Ten **Commandments** and made a **covenant** with them to be their God if they would do as he said. Moses died on Mount Nebo before the Israelites entered the Promised Land. For a long time, Moses was mistakenly regarded as the human author of the first five books of the Bible, which contain many Jewish laws.

A famous statue of Moses is the one in Rome carved by Michelangelo. It shows Moses with horns because the Bible says that when he came down from the mountain carrying the Law, he was radiant. The word *radiant* was mistranslated as "horns."

Mystical Body of Christ

The word *mystical* means "spiritual, not being able to be perceived by our five senses." The Mystical Body of Christ is the **Church**. Jesus is the head, and we are the members. He explained that we share life just like a vine and its branches. Receiving the **Eucharist** unites us with Christ and the other members. Just as the members of our body carry out different functions, we each have our own function in the Mystical Body of Christ.

N

nave

The nave is the center area of the church from the entrance to the **sanctuary**. It is where the congregation worships.

New Testament

See **Bible**.

Nicene Creed

The Nicene Creed is a statement of beliefs that we pray at Mass. It was first written by the Council of Nicaea in 325 in response to the Arian heresy, which claimed that Jesus was not equal to the Father. In 381, the Council of Constantinople reworked the Nicene Creed, mostly by adding to it. Therefore, this creed is more accurately called the Nicene-Constantinople Creed.

novena

Novem is Latin for "nine." A novena is nine consecutive periods of **prayer**. A novena prayer is usually prayed nine days in a row. But it can also be prayed nine hours in a row or once a week for nine weeks. This custom comes from the nine days that the Apostles and Mary prayed together in a room in Jerusalem before the Holy Spirit came. Novenas are prayed for a specific intention or in honor of Jesus or a saint.

novice

Anyone beginning something new is a novice. In a religious community, a novice is a person in an early stage of formation. This stage is called the novitiate. During that time, the novice learns about religious life, and the community learns if the novice is qualified for it. After a year or two, the novice may make temporary **vows**.

nun

Strictly speaking, a nun is a woman religious who makes **vows**, lives in community, and prays the **Liturgy of the Hours** in common. Unlike an apostolic woman religious (called a sister) who carries on ministries in the world, a "cloistered" (enclosed) nun usually remains in the convent or monastery. She seeks union with God, prays, and does **penance**. Sisters are commonly referred to as nuns.

nuncio

A nuncio is an archbishop appointed by the **pope** to be his representative or ambassador to a country. He is also called the papal nuncio or apostolic nuncio. The nuncio's offices (embassy) are called the apostolic nunciature. In the United States, the nunciature is located in Washington, D.C.

O

L'Osservatore Romano

L' Osservatore Romano (*The Roman Observer*) is the daily newspaper of the **Holy See**. It reports on the pope's public activities and the Church around the world, and it publishes articles by scholars. A weekly edition is published in different languages.

O Antiphons

When you sing the hymn "O Come, O Come Emmanuel," you are singing a paraphrase of the O Antiphons. The O Antiphons are short prayers that are prayed in Evening Prayer (Vespers) on the seven days before Christmas Eve. They each begin with O and address Jesus by a title. Each antiphon refers to a prophecy of Isaiah about the **Messiah**. The titles in the O Antiphons are *Wisdom*, *Lord*, *Root of Jesse*, *Key of David*, *Dayspring*, *King of Nations*, and *Emmanuel*. In Latin, the initials of these words spelled backward is *Ero cras*, which means "Tomorrow I will come."

octave

In music an octave is eight notes in a row. A religious octave is eight days of celebration for a feast. It includes the feast itself and the seven days following it. Catholics observe the octave of Christmas and the octave of Easter. The Week of Prayer for Church Unity (January 18–25) was originally called the Church Unity Octave.

Old Testament

See **Bible**.

omnipotence

If something, like medicine, is potent, it is strong. Omnipotence is the attribute or quality of God that means all-powerful or almighty. God has infinite (unlimited) power. He can do anything as long as it doesn't contradict his nature or is absurd, such as making a square circle.

omnipresence

Omnipresence means being everywhere. It is one of God's attributes or qualities. God is a pure spirit, unlimited by space. He is fully present in all places all the time. How comforting to know that God is always with us as our loving Creator. Psalm 139:1–12 is a beautiful prayer about God's abiding presence.

omniscience

Omniscience means all-knowing. It is one of God's attributes or qualities. God knows all things. His knowledge is eternal: he knows the past, present, and the future. Jesus said that our Father knows when a sparrow falls to the ground. He even knows the number of hairs on our head. (Matthew 10:29–30) God also knows what is in our hearts.

ordination

Ordination is the consecration of men to be ministers for worship and for the sanctification of God's people. It is administered by a **bishop** through the laying on of hands and the prayer of consecration. Jesus conferred the priesthood upon the **Apostles** at the Last Supper. The Sacrament of **Holy Orders** has three forms: the diaconate, priesthood, and episcopate.

ordo

How do priests know what Mass to celebrate or when Easter starts each year? The ordo is a booklet that gives the dates of the liturgical seasons and feasts. For each day it tells the rank of the feast and the **liturgical color** to use at Mass. The ordo is published every year as a guide for Mass and for praying the **Liturgy of the Hours**.

Original Sin

People sometimes wonder why there is suffering in the world. It is because of Original Sin, the first sin. This sin was committed by the first two human beings, **Adam** and **Eve**. In the Book of **Genesis**, the Original Sin was disobeying God's order not to eat the fruit of a certain tree. **Satan**, appearing in the form of a snake, persuaded Eve to eat the fruit, and she persuaded Adam to eat it. This disobedience destroyed the friendship between God and his human creatures. Adam and Eve lost their life with God, their special powers were weakened, and they became subject to death.

This event is called the Fall because our first parents fell from grace and God's friendship. The consequences of Original Sin were passed on to all the descendants of Adam and Eve. Jesus made up for all sin by his death on the cross. Now through Baptism we receive the **supernatural** life of **grace** again and become children of God. We can hope for eternal life.

See Genesis 3:1–24 for the story of the Fall.

Our Father

See **Lord's Prayer**.

Our Lady

You have probably heard the name Notre Dame. It is the French translation of Our Lady, which is a title for the Blessed Virgin **Mary**. It is
similar to the title Our Lord for Jesus. Other titles of Mary begin with
Our Lady, such as Our Lady of Ransom, Our Lady of Good Counsel,
and Our Lady of Fatima.

P

pall

1) A pall is a stiff, square board covered with linen that is placed over
the **chalice** at Mass. It blocks dust and insects from the wine.
2) At funeral Masses the cloth spread over the coffin is called a pall. It
is usually white to recall the white garment of Baptism, and it represents faith in the Resurrection. Often it has a **cross** on it, for the cross
conquered death.

pallium

A pallium is a vestment worn by the pope and certain archbishops
that symbolizes authority. Worn around the shoulders, it is a narrow,
circular band with a strip hanging in the front and back. Six black
crosses decorate it. A pallium is made in part from the wool of two
lambs blessed in the Church of St. Agnes in Rome on the feast of
Saint Agnes.

palm

A palm is a **sacramental** when it is blessed on **Passion Sunday**, which
is the beginning of **Holy Week**. On that day, it is distributed at Mass
to commemorate Christ's triumphant entry into **Jerusalem** when the
people spread palm branches before him. At some churches people
walk in procession holding the palms and singing a song hailing Christ
as king. Palms are placed in homes, sometimes after being fashioned

into crosses, flowers, or other shapes. Blessed palms are burned to make the ashes that are used on **Ash Wednesday**.

Palm Sunday

See **Passion Sunday**.

papacy

1) The papacy is a reference to the office of the pope as head of the whole Church or as the ruler of the **Vatican** State.

2) The years of a pope's reign are referred to as his papacy.

papal blessing

The papal (or apostolic) **blessing** is a special blessing given by the pope, for example, the *Urbi et Orbi* blessing. It has a plenary **indulgence**, which means it remits temporal punishment for sins. We may ask for a papal blessing for ourselves or for a loved one to mark a special occasion, such as an anniversary. Usually the petition is submitted along with an offering through the diocesan **chancery** office. After a few months, we receive a parchment that testifies that the pope has given his blessing. At times bishops and priests may be delegated to give apostolic blessings.

papal flag

The papal flag is the flag of the **Vatican**. It is a square with two vertical bands, yellow on the left and white on the right. In the center of the white band is the seal of the Vatican State, which consists of the papal triple tiara above two crossed keys. One key is silver to symbolize the pope's civil authority, and the other is gold for his spiritual authority. The keys represent the keys of Heaven that Jesus entrusted to **Peter**. In churches the papal flag is usually displayed next to the national flag.

parable

A parable is a teaching device that Jesus often used in which a comparison is made. The parables of Jesus convey a **supernatural** truth through natural images: ordinary objects and familiar actions. They are usually short stories that reveal something about God and the **Kingdom of God**. Through parables, Jesus led people to a new way of thinking and acting.

See Luke 10:29 for one of the most famous parables, the Good Samaritan.

Paraclete

The word *Paraclete* literally means "called to stand beside." It is a Greek term found in the Gospel of John that is translated as *counselor, comforter,* or *advocate*. Our first Paraclete is Jesus. At the **Last Supper** he promised another Paraclete, namely the **Holy Spirit**. This Third Person of the Trinity is present with us and within us, guiding us and making us holy.

Paradise

See **Heaven, Eden**.

parish

Your Christian life is grounded and nourished at your parish. A parish is a community of **Catholics** within a **diocese** who worship at the same church. It is led by a **pastor**, who is appointed by the bishop. The pastor may be assisted by one or more priests called **parochial vicars** as well as a **parish council**. Parish staff, which includes **pastoral associates**, also ministers to the needs of the parishioners. Parishes are usually formed according to geography.

parish council

A parish council is a group of parishioners who assist the **pastor**. They give him advice on matters related to parish life. The members are usually elected by the parish.

parishioner

A parishioner is a registered member of a **parish**, usually one that is near his or her house. An active parishioner not only benefits from the **sacraments** provided by the parish but participates in parish activities and contributes to its support.

parochial vicar

A parochial vicar is a parish priest who assists the **pastor** in ministering to the parishioners. He is appointed by the bishop. Formerly, parochial vicars were called associate pastors.

parousia (par-OO-see-a)

The Greek word *parousia* means "arrival" or "presence." Parousia is the second coming of **Christ** to earth. His coming in glory will be his victory and will bring about the fullness of the **Kingdom of God**. At that time Christ will judge all people.

See Matthew 25:31–46 for Jesus' description of the judgment of nations.

Paschal Candle

The Paschal, or **Easter** Candle, is the large white candle that is decorated and lit at the Easter Vigil. It is also called the Christ Candle because it stands for the light of Christ. The priest carves the **Alpha and Omega** and a **cross** with a numeral of the year in each quadrant. He embeds five grains of **incense** into the candle to symbolize the five wounds of Jesus. The congregation's candles are then lit from its flame. The Paschal Candle remains lit throughout the Easter season and for Baptisms and funerals.

Paschal Mystery

The Paschal Mystery is the Passion, Death, **Resurrection**, and **Ascension** of Jesus that brought about our **Salvation**. We participate in and celebrate this mystery at every Eucharist. *Pasch* is another name for

Passover, the Jewish feast that recalls God's saving action at the beginning of the Exodus. A lamb was sacrificed and its blood marking the doorways resulted in death "passing over" the Jewish houses. The lamb was then eaten. This *Pasch* foreshadowed the Christian Paschal Mystery when the **sacrifice** of Jesus, the Lamb of God, saved the world from eternal death. Jesus' death, when he passed over from this life to the Father, occurred at the time of the Jewish Passover. We celebrate the Paschal Mystery during the **Easter Triduum**.

Passion of Jesus

The Passion includes all the sufferings, physical and mental, that Jesus underwent for us. It culminates with his death on the cross. The Passion of Jesus led to glory for him and to **Salvation** for us. The four Gospel accounts of the suffering of Jesus are called Passion Narratives. They are read during **Holy Week**.

Passion Sunday (Palm Sunday)

Passion Sunday is the Sunday before **Easter** and the beginning of **Holy Week**. It is also called Palm Sunday. On this day palms are blessed, and people may walk with them in the processional to commemorate Christ's triumphal entry into Jerusalem. The Gospel reading is an account of the Passion and Death of Jesus.

pastor

A pastor is the priest appointed by the bishop to be the head of a **parish**. He takes care of the spiritual needs of his people by providing the **sacraments**, teaching, and giving advice. He also administers the parish buildings and finances. It comes from the Latin word for "shepherd."

pastoral associate

A pastoral associate is a layperson or religious who serves a parish by caring for the needs of parishioners.

pastoral ministry

Pastoral ministry is all the ways that the people in the Church are cared for. Priests and **deacons** carry out pastoral ministry as well as **laypeople** who are trained.

paten

A paten is the plate that holds the large **host** during Mass. It is a sacred vessel consecrated with **Chrism** and often made of gold or silver.

patriarch/matriarch

1) A patriarch is a leader and forefather of the Israelites. **Abraham,** Isaac, Jacob, and Jacob's twelve sons are commonly identified as patriarchs. Sometimes fathers going back to **Adam** are also given that title. The wives of the patriarchs are called matriarchs.

2) The highest-ranking leader in the Eastern Christian Churches, a bishop, is also known as a patriarch. His Church is a patriarchate.

patron saint

A patron **saint** is someone in Heaven who intercedes for a person, place, or organization. It is often the saint for whom the person, place, or organization is named. Saints are often charged with praying for people in particular occupations or for things that are related to their own lives. For example, Saint Martha, who prepared a meal for Jesus and the **Apostles**, is the patron saint of cooks. Saint Patrick is the patron saint of Ireland because he was a **missionary** there. The pope or popular acclaim may determine a saint's responsibility.

Paul

Chances are that at Mass next Sunday you will hear something written by Saint Paul. He is called the **Apostle** to the **Gentiles** because he brought the **Good News** to them. As a Pharisee named Saul, he persecuted Christians. But on the way to Damascus, Paul encountered the risen Jesus who asked, "Why do you persecute me?" Paul became a devoted Christian. During three missionary journeys around the Mediterranean Sea, he preached the Gospel to Jews and Gentiles. He founded churches and wrote letters explaining the faith and encouraging the new Christians. Many of his letters, called **Epistles**, are in the New Testament. Paul endured much suffering for his faith in Christ and eventually was imprisoned in Rome and beheaded. Accounts of his life and work are in the **Acts of the Apostles**.

Penance

1) The Sacrament of Penance is a **Sacrament** of Healing in which sins are forgiven through a **priest** who acts on behalf of Jesus. Another name for this sacrament is Reconciliation because it repairs the damage that sin has done to our relationship with God and other Church members. **Contrition**, the confession of sins, and the intention to sin no more are required for **absolution**. **Mortal sins** must be confessed. But confessing **venial sins** is also recommended because it strengthens our spiritual life. The sacrament gives us **grace** to resist temptation. The priest assigns a **penance**, a prayer or a good work, as a means to make up for sin and to keep us from future sin.

The sacrament has three forms. The usual form is individual confession, which may be carried out face-to-face. Another form is with several people praying together. In this case confession and absolution are still individual. A rare form is general absolution, which is given to a group when individual confessions are impossible. The situation must be extreme, for example, danger of death. The diocesan bishop must give permission for general absolution or be informed of it later. Confession of mortal sins individually is still required afterward if possible. Mortal sins must be confessed at least once a year and always before receiving Holy Communion.

We prepare for the Sacrament of Penance by making an **examination of conscience** and being sorry for our sins. The priest is bound not to reveal sins confessed to him. This is known as the **seal of confession.**

2) A penance is the prayer, good works, or acts of self-denial done to make up for sin and to grow holier. The priest assigns a penance in the Sacrament of Penance.

Pentateuch

The Pentateuch is the first five books of the **Bible.** Jewish people call them the Torah, which means "the Law." For centuries it was thought that **Moses** was the author. Today we believe that the books were woven together from different strands of oral tradition. The Pentateuch contains stories of Creation, the early people, and the **Exodus.** It also lists Mosaic laws.

Pentecost

Pentecost is the feast that celebrates the descent of the **Holy Spirit** on the **Church** just as Jesus promised. It is commonly referred to as the birthday of the Church. The **Acts of the Apostles** describes how the **disciples** and **Mary** were gathered in prayer when the room was filled with the sound of a strong wind and tongues of fire rested over their heads. The disciples spoke in tongues so that people from different areas could understand them. Peter gave a sermon that led to about three thousand people being baptized that day. All these events occurred on the Jewish feast of Pentecost, which was a harvest feast fifty days after Passover. We celebrate Pentecost fifty days after Easter.

See Acts of the Apostles 2:1–41 for the story of Pentecost.

Peter

Peter is the **Apostle** whom Jesus appointed as leader of the **Church,** the first pope. His original name was Simon, but Jesus called him Peter, which means "rock." Jesus declared, "Upon this rock I will build my church. . . . I will give you the keys to the kingdom of heaven" (Matthew 16:18–19). Peter, a fisherman, and his brother, Andrew, were the first men called to be Apostles. Peter usually spoke for all of them, and he was one of three Apostles whom Jesus chose to be with him at the Transfiguration, the raising of Jairus's daughter, and the Agony in the Garden. In the **Acts of the Apostles**, Peter clearly appears as the Church leader. However, Peter was not without faults. He was impetuous. He contradicted Jesus when Jesus spoke of his death. He asked Jesus to let him walk on water but then grew afraid. He objected when Jesus wanted to wash his feet. In the Garden of Gethsemane, he cut off the ear of Malchus, the servant of the high priest. Worse, when Jesus was captured, Peter denied knowing him three times. Still, after the Resurrection, Jesus led Peter to declare his love for him three times. And each time Jesus told Peter to feed his lambs or his sheep.

According to legend, Peter was martyred on a cross. He asked to be crucified upside down because he was not worthy to die as Jesus did. Peter is buried under the Basilica of Saint Peter in Rome, which is one of the largest churches in the world. In the Bible, there are two letters that are attributed to Peter.

See John 21:15–19 for the story of Jesus charging Peter to care for his Church.

pew

For centuries people stood for church services. Then in the fifteenth century, pews became popular. A pew is a church bench where members of the congregation sit and kneel. It is usually long and wooden. Kneelers and holders for **missalettes** and hymnals may be attached.

Pharisees

The Pharisees were religious leaders of the Jewish people at the time of Jesus. They were mostly laymen who promoted the keeping of all Jewish laws. Unlike the **Sadducees**, other Jewish leaders, Pharisees believed in **angels** and in **resurrection** after death. The Gospels portray the Pharisees as men who resented Jesus for breaking the religious laws and claiming equality with God. They tried to trick him into saying something that would turn people against him. Jesus scolded them for being hypocrites, that is, for only observing the law outwardly.

pilgrimage

A pilgrimage is a journey to a holy place to honor God or a saint, to do **penance**, to ask a favor, or to give thanks for something. The person who makes a pilgrimage is called a pilgrim. People make pilgrimages to the Holy Land, to Rome, and to shrines where the Blessed Virgin Mary has appeared. Some pilgrimages may earn an **indulgence**.

pontiff

Pontiff is a title for the Holy Father. It means "bridge builder." The **pope** is the bridge on earth between God and human beings. He is also called the Supreme Pontiff.

pope

The pope is the visible head of the Church on earth and the **Bishop of Rome**. He represents Jesus, the head of the Church. The word *pope* comes from the Greek and Latin words for "father." The pope is the supreme authority over the universal Church. He is the successor of Saint Peter, to whom Jesus entrusted the leadership of his Church. The pope is also the ruler of **Vatican** City, the smallest state in the world. Like every bishop, he has a motto and a coat of arms.

The pope speaks out for justice, peace, and morality. He writes letters called **encyclicals** on pertinent issues. Occasionally, the pope calls together his fellow bishops in an **ecumenical council** or a **synod** to assist in formulating Church doctrine, policy, and customs. The pope resides in the Vatican in Rome, where the offices of the **Roman Curia** are located. A pope is elected by **cardinals** in a closed meeting called a **conclave**. There have been more than 260 popes. Titles for the pope include **Holy Father**, Vicar of Christ, Supreme Pontiff, His Holiness, and Servant of the Servants of God.

possession

Possession is **Satan's** influence over a person's mind and body. The devil is cast out through prayers invoking the power of Jesus in a process called an exorcism. This is performed with the approval of the bishop by an exorcist, a specially-trained priest. The Gospels tell of many times when Jesus cast out evil spirits. Some behavior assumed to be the result of possession is in fact a symptom of mental illness. Consequently, an exorcism is carried out only after a medical examination of the person.

postulant

A postulant is a person who has been accepted by a religious community as a possible member. For at least six months, the postulant experiences religious life. After this period, he or she may enter the **novitiate**, which is the next stage of formation.

prayer

Prayer is raising the mind and heart to God. It is thinking about God, speaking to him, and listening to him. The First Commandment requires us to pray. Prayer can be vocal or mental. It can be a set formula or spontaneous. **Meditation** and **contemplation** are two forms of prayer. In prayer we adore God, thank him, ask for something for ourselves or others, or express sorrow for sin. In two **parables**, Jesus taught us not to give up praying for something. (Luke 11:5–8 and Luke 18:1–8) He assured us that our Father will answer our prayers if we have faith.

Jesus is a good model of prayer. He prayed alone (sometimes all night) and with others. He prayed in the Temple and before major events in his life. When the Apostles asked Jesus to teach them how to pray, he gave us the **Lord's Prayer**. The Mass is our greatest prayer. We can also pray to Mary and the saints. Prayer is as important to our spiritual life as breathing is to our bodily life.

Precepts of the Church

The Precepts of the Church, sometimes called the Commandments of the Church, are rules for its members. They are the minimum requirements that Catholics should follow. The *Catechism of the Catholic Church* lists these five precepts:

1. Attend Mass on Sundays and **Holy Days of Obligation**.
2. Confess serious sin at least once a year.
3. Receive Holy Communion at least once a year during the Easter season.
4. Observe the days of **fasting** and **abstinence**.
5. Provide for the needs of the Church.

prelate

A prelate is an ordained man who holds a special position in the Church. The main prelates are the **pope**, **cardinals**, **bishops**, and **abbots**.

Presentation

Forty days after Jesus' birth, Mary and Joseph took him to the Temple and presented him to God. This was to comply with the Mosaic Law that held that firstborn sons had to be redeemed back from God. During the presentation of Jesus, Simeon recognized him as the **Messiah** and declared him as the light to the **Gentiles**. He also foretold conflict for Jesus and sorrow for Mary. The elderly widow Anna was there too and was privileged to meet the Messiah. We celebrate the Presentation on February 2. On this day, which is called Candlemas Day, candles are blessed. The Presentation is the Fourth Joyful Mystery of the Rosary.

priest/presbyter

A priest in general is someone who offers a **sacrifice**. Jesus is the greatest priest. He sacrificed himself for the **Salvation** of the world. A

Catholic priest is a man ordained by a bishop to offer the **Eucharist** and provide the other **sacraments** to the people of God. He is called Father, usually works in a parish, and wears a white Roman collar. Priesthood (the presbyterate) is the second level of orders between the diaconate and the episcopate. A priest is first a deacon, and a bishop is first a priest. Another name for a priest is presbyter. Priests are trained in a school called a seminary. The house they live in is called a rectory. Through Baptism we can share in the priesthood of Jesus and offer ourselves with him at Mass.

prior/prioress

A prior is the superior, or leader, of a **monastery** or **abbey** in some men's religious orders. A prioress is a religious leader in some women's religious orders. The house of such religious orders is called a priory.

prophet

We usually think of a prophet as a person who foretells the future. A prophet is actually someone who speaks for God, not necessarily someone who makes predictions. Old Testament prophets constantly called the Israelites to repent and keep their **covenant** with God. They delivered messages by written or spoken word or by symbolic actions. **Moses** was a great prophet. Eighteen books in the Bible are the writings of prophets. Isaiah, Jeremiah, Ezekiel, and Daniel are known as the major prophets because their books are the longest. Some prophecies speak of the coming **Messiah**. **John the Baptist**, who prepared people for Jesus, was the last Old Testament prophet. **Jesus** was the prophet who, more than anyone else, spoke for God and revealed him. Through our Baptism we share in Christ's role of prophet. We too are to speak forth the Word of God.

Providence, Divine

What some people call a happy coincidence may really be providence. Divine Providence is God's plan for the universe and its fulfillment.

God governs and cares for all things wisely and lovingly. Jesus taught that our heavenly Father, who cares for the birds of the air and the flowers of the field, cares even more for us.

See Matthew 6:25–34 and Matthew 10:29–31 for Jesus' lessons about providence.

psalm

At every Mass we pray a Responsorial Psalm before the Gospel. A psalm is a song-prayer in praise of God. The Book of Psalms contains 150 psalms. King **David**, who played the harp, is traditionally regarded as the composer. The Jewish people prayed psalms in and on the way to the Temple. Jesus and Mary prayed them. Many psalms are laments, which are complaints to God. Other psalms give thanks to God or express sorrow for sin. The shortest psalm is Psalm 117, and the longest is Psalm 119, which is about the importance of God's law.

The psalms have the characteristics of Hebrew poetry. Lines are repeated with the same or similar words. There are many figures of speech, such as metaphors and similes. For example, God is compared to a rock and enemies are like bees. Some hymns that we sing are psalms set to modern music.

pulpit

See **ambo.**

Purgatory

Purgatory is the state of people who have died but are not yet worthy to be in God's presence because of their sins. It is a place of purification that cleanses them of their **venial sins** and faults and remits temporal punishment that is a result of sin. Purgatory will exist only until the end of the world. We may pray for those in Purgatory in order to shorten their time there. As members of the **Communion of Saints,** they are more aptly referred to as holy souls than poor souls.

November 2 is the Feast of All Souls when we pray for the people in Purgatory.

purificator

A purificator is a white linen cloth used to wipe the **chalice** as it is offered to communicants. This cloth is also used to dry the sacred vessels after Holy Communion. It is folded in thirds and may have a red cross in the center. A purificator is not blessed.

pyx (PIKS)

1) A pyx is a small, round, metal container in which sacred **hosts** are placed to be taken to the sick.

2) Pyx is another name for the luna, the vessel in the **tabernacle** that holds the large sacred host that is placed in the monstrance for exposition.

Q

Q document

The **Gospel** of Mark is thought to be the first Gospel written, from which Matthew and Luke drew material. But some words of Jesus found in the Gospels of Matthew and Luke are not found in the Gospel of Mark or are different. The existence of the Q document is a theory proposed by some Scripture scholars to explain these differences. The Q document is an unknown collection of sayings of Jesus that may be the source of these quotations. The Q stands for the German word *quelle*, which means "source."

Queenship of Mary

In 1954, Pope Pius XII gave **Mary** the title of queen. She is the Queen of Heaven and Earth. Mary was called queen as early as the fourth century. This is a logical title for her because she is the Mother of Jesus, who is king. A **May crowning** is a ritual honoring Mary in which her image is crowned. The Queenship of Mary is celebrated on August 22, the octave after the Feast of the Assumption.

R

Real Presence

The Real Presence is the **doctrine** that the **Eucharist** truly is Jesus Christ, body and blood, soul and divinity. The Eucharist is not a symbol of Jesus, or Jesus only in the spiritual sense. He is actually there in substance, and he is there entirely.

Reconciliation

See **Penance**.

rectory

A rectory is the house where parish priests live. It is usually on the same grounds as the church where they minister.

redemption

Redemption is the **Salvation** of the human race by the Passion, Death, and **Resurrection** of Jesus. **Sin** caused the loss of **grace** and friendship with God, death, and the loss of eternal life for the human race. In the past, slaves could be freed if someone redeemed them, that is, paid to set them free. Sin made us captives of Satan. Through his death, Jesus redeemed us. That is, he freed us by paying with his life. Our redeemer restored us to grace and eternal life. We have been justified and are again children of God and heirs of Heaven.

Regina Coeli

Regina Coeli is Latin for "Queen of Heaven." The *Regina Coeli* is a prayer about the Resurrection in which we address Mary as Queen of Heaven. We pray it at Easter in place of the **Angelus** during the day and in the **Liturgy of the Hours**.

relics

People treasure keepsakes from deceased family members. Relics are mementos of a **saint** that are venerated. There are three levels. A first-class relic is the saint's body or a part of it. A second-class relic is part of the clothing or anything used by the saint. A third-class relic is an object that has been touched to a first-class relic. We venerate the relic by bowing to it, kissing it, or kissing our fingers and touching it. Relics may not be sold. It is a tradition to have first-class relics placed under the **altar** of a church. A relic is kept in a **reliquary**.

reliquary

A reliquary is a holder for a **relic**. It may be made of precious metals and highly decorated. Reliquaries often have a window through which the relic can be viewed.

reparation

See **restitution**.

repentance

Repentance is sorrow for sin and a change of heart for the good. God constantly calls people to repent. Old Testament **prophets**, **John the Baptist**, and Jesus urged people to give up sin and return to God. When we repent, we confess our sins, express our sorrow, and ask forgiveness in the Sacrament of **Penance**. We also intend not to sin again.

requiem

Requiem describes a Mass that is offered for a deceased person. The term comes from the first word in Latin of the prayer for the dead that begins "Eternal rest grant unto them."

Reservation of the Blessed Sacrament

Reservation of the **Blessed Sacrament** is the practice of keeping sacred hosts in a tabernacle in a church or chapel. This allows us to visit Jesus in the Blessed Sacrament and pray. It also makes the hosts available for taking to the sick.

restitution

Restitution, or reparation, is making up for a harm done. This could be returning to the rightful owner something stolen or repairing damage deliberately caused. If it isn't possible to compensate the victim for the loss, an equivalent amount of money can be donated to charity. Justice and **absolution** require **restitution** in addition to true **contrition**.

resurrection (in general)

Resurrection is the returning to life from the dead, both body and soul. It is a doctrine of our faith that we profess in the **Creed**. At the end of time all people who have died will rise, be judged, and learn their eternal destiny: **Heaven** or **Hell**.

Resurrection of Jesus

The Resurrection is the mystery of Jesus rising from the dead three days after his death on the cross. It is his victory over death and the completion of our **redemption**. The Church has always believed in the Resurrection as a chief **doctrine**. The **Gospels** testify to it, although their accounts differ, and Saint **Peter** preached it. The risen Jesus has a glorified body, which is not bound by time or space. He appeared to many of his **disciples**. Because Jesus rose from the dead, we can believe his words that we too may someday enjoy eternal life. We celebrate the Resurrection of Jesus on Easter. It is our greatest feast.

See Matthew 28:1–10 for one Gospel account of the Resurrection.

retreat

A retreat is a period of time spent in quiet and prayer to renew one's spiritual life. It is usually led by a director who gives talks or has personal conferences with retreatants, or both. There is often an opportunity for daily Mass and the Sacrament of Penance. Retreat houses offer various retreats throughout the year. Days of recollection are mini-retreats that last a day or part of a day.

Revelation

1) Divine Revelation is God's making himself and his plan known to us. It is divine self-communication. God has revealed himself through the **prophets** and through **Scripture** and **Tradition**. In Jesus, we have the full and direct revelation of God.

2) The Book of Revelation is the last book of the Bible, which is also sometimes called the Apocalypse. It describes John's visions of Heaven and the last days as a means of offering hope to persecuted Christians. It reminds them and us that in the end God will triumph.

rite

1) A rite is the words and actions of a liturgical event—for example, the Rite of **Baptism**.

2) A rite is one of the historic liturgies that developed in the Catholic Church. Besides the Roman (or Latin) Rite, there are others that originated in different cultures, such as the Byzantine Rite and the Maronite Rite.

Rite of Christian Initiation of Adults (RCIA)

People who wish to join the Catholic Church go through a period of formation with the help of a **sponsor**. The Rite of Christian Initiation of Adults is the four-stage process by which adults become members of the Catholic Church. First is the precatechumenate, the inquiry stage. Second is the catechumenate, when the candidates are called catechumens and leave Mass after the Gospel for instruction. During this stage the catechumens concentrate on learning about the Catholic faith and forming their spiritual lives. Third is the election stage, which starts on the First Sunday of Lent. It includes rituals during the Sunday Masses: scrutinies (prayers for the catechumens' growth in holiness), the presentation of the Our Father and the Creed, and anointing. The final stage is the initiation at the Easter Vigil by the celebration of Baptism, Confirmation, and First Holy Communion.

Roman Catholic

1) Roman Catholic is the name of the Church founded by Jesus that has the pope, the Bishop of Rome, as its head. When the Protestant churches formed, the term Roman Catholic became more prevalent to distinguish the **Catholic Church** under the pope from these other Christian churches. The term as used today encompasses the one Western Church and the 22 **Eastern Churches**.

2) A Roman Catholic is a person who belongs to the Roman Catholic Church.

Roman congregations

Roman Congregations are nine departments in the **Roman Curia** that help the pope govern the **Church**. A **cardinal** and a secretary, who is usually an archbishop, are the heads of each congregation. There are congregations for the doctrine of the faith, Eastern Churches, divine worship and sacraments, causes of saints, **evangelization** of peoples, clergy, bishops, consecrated life and societies of apostolic life, Catholic education, and bishops.

Roman Curia

The Roman Curia is the body that assists the Holy Father in governing the Church. It is composed of the nine **Roman congregations**, the Secretariat of State, and various other commissions, offices, and councils.

Roman Missal

See **missal/missalette**.

Rosary

Catholics are known for praying the Rosary. Often Catholics are buried with a rosary in their hands. The Rosary is a devotion in honor of **Mary** that combines the recitation of prayers with mental prayer. A circle of beads is used to keep track of the prayers. We pray the Hail Mary on beads arranged in five sets of ten, called decades. We begin each decade with an Our Father and end it with a Glory Be to the Father. During each decade we reflect on a mystery, an event in the lives of Jesus and Mary. Therefore, the Rosary can be called the Gospel on beads. There are four sets of mysteries: Joyful, Luminous, Sorrowful, and Glorious.

We begin the Rosary by making the Sign of the Cross with the crucifix that is attached and then praying the Apostles' Creed. Then we pray an Our Father, three Hail Marys, and a Glory Be on the beads after the **crucifix**. Some people pray the Rosary on one-decade rings or bracelets. We can always pray the Rosary on something readily available—our ten fingers! When Mary has appeared on earth, she has urged us to pray the Rosary as penance and for peace.

The Rosary began when illiterate Christians could not pray the one hundred and fifty psalms. Instead they prayed that many Our Fathers on beads. Later this practice evolved into one hundred and fifty Hail Marys. Saint Dominic is associated with the Rosary because the order he founded promoted it. Father Patrick Peyton (1909–1992), the Holy Cross priest who founded The Family Rosary Crusade, encouraged families to pray the Rosary together. He said, "The family that prays together stays together."

S

Sabbath

The Sabbath was the seventh day of the week, Saturday, when the Jews worshiped and rested. It began on Friday evening. The Sabbath originated with the **Genesis** account of Creation in which God rested on the seventh day. To keep the Sabbath was to obey the Fourth **Commandment** to keep the Lord's Day holy. Jewish writings forbade thirty-nine kinds of work on the Sabbath, which religious leaders expanded so that "work" included such things as tying or untying a rope, lighting a fire, using medicine, and walking more than three thousand feet. Jesus was criticized by the Jewish leaders for not following all the Sabbath regulations.

Christians moved the observance of the Sabbath to Sunday in honor of the Lord's **Resurrection**. On this day we celebrate the Eucharist. Instead of working, we spend the day enjoying our family and creation, visiting friends and relatives, engaging in hobbies or sports, performing acts of charity, and praying.

sacrament

A sacrament is a sign we can sense (see, hear, and so on) instituted by Jesus that confers the **grace** it signifies. There are seven sacraments. **Baptism, Confirmation**, and the **Eucharist** are the Sacraments of Initiation. **Penance** and the **Anointing of the Sick** are the Sacraments of Healing. **Holy Orders** and **Matrimony** are the Sacraments of Service or Vocation. The ritual (words and actions) of a sacrament brings about the grace. It is not caused by the holiness of the minister or of the person celebrating the sacrament. Baptism is required to receive the other sacraments. The Eucharist is the queen of all the sacraments. Each sacrament confers a particular grace called sacramental grace. The **Eastern Churches** call the sacraments *mysteries*.

sacramental

A sacramental is a sacred sign related to the **sacraments** that obtains grace through the merits and prayers of the **Church**. Some sacramentals are objects, such as holy water, sacred vessels, **rosaries**, and **medals**. And some are actions, such as **blessings** and **consecrations**. The effect a sacramental has depends on the attitude of the person using it. This is not like the sacraments, which are effective in themselves.

Sacramentary

See **missal/missalette**.

sacrarium

A sacrarium is a sink that drains directly into the ground and is used for washing sacred vessels and linens. It is normally found in the **sacristy**.

Sacred Heart

In our culture a heart stands for life, love, and our whole being. The Sacred Heart is a symbol of God's total, tremendous love for us. God's love compelled him to become human and die to save us. After Jesus died, a soldier thrust a lance into his heart. In art, the Sacred Heart is depicted as a heart surmounted by a cross and encircled with thorns. Flames shoot forth from the heart to represent the burning love Jesus has for us. In some pictures, Jesus is shown offering his Sacred Heart to us.

Devotion to the Sacred Heart began in the eleventh century. **Monks** and others included it in their private prayers. Then in the seventeenth century, Jesus appeared to Saint Margaret Mary Alacoque and asked her to promote this devotion. He said he wanted everyone to know the depths of his love. He lamented, "Behold this heart, which has so loved men [and women], but which is so little loved in return." Jesus requested frequent Communion, especially on the first Friday of each month; holy hours; and a feast in honor of his Sacred Heart. The pope established the Solemnity of the Sacred Heart, which is on the Friday nineteen days after Pentecost. People wear Sacred Heart scapulars or badges. Families are consecrated to the Sacred Heart, and his image is enthroned in their homes. Some Catholics receive Holy Communion on nine consecutive Fridays. The Litany to the Sacred Heart addresses the Heart of Jesus thirty-three times, one for each year of his life.

sacrifice

1) A sacrifice is a gift offered to God to express adoration and thanksgiving or to make up for a **sin**. In the time of the Old Testament, people gave God part of their harvest and livestock. Holocausts were offerings that were set on fire to show they were God's alone. Sometimes the sacrifice was eaten. Some sacrifices were carried out to confirm a **covenant**. The Temple in Jerusalem was the place of sacrifice for the Jews until it was destroyed.

Jesus called his death on the cross a sacrifice for a New Covenant. He was the high priest and the victim who made up for all sins. He offered himself at the Last Supper at Passover, when lambs were sacrificed to save the Jews. At each **Eucharist** the sacrifice of Jesus is reenacted.

2) To sacrifice something is to do without it for the sake of a greater good. It is self-denial. For example, during **Lent** we might sacrifice playing our favorite computer game to make up for our sins and to grow in self-control. We can also sacrifice our time to do works of **charity**.

sacrilege

A sacrilege is the disrespectful treatment of a sacred person, place, or thing. Receiving a **sacrament** unworthily is also a sacrilege. Committing a sacrilege is a sin contrary to the **virtue** of religion by which we worship God.

sacristan

See **sacristy**.

sacristy

A sacristy is the room in a church where the **clergy** vests for worship. In it are stored sacred vessels, vestments, and other items needed for worship. A **sacrarium** is usually there. The person in charge of the sacristy is called the *sacristan*.

Sadducees

The Sadducees were a priestly class of Jews at the time of Jesus. These wealthy and educated men held seats in the **Sanhedrin**, the ruling body. They also were friendly with the Roman government. Unlike the **Pharisees**, the Sadducees did not believe in angels or the resurrection of the body. They opposed Jesus and his Church.

saint

Sometimes a person is referred to as a living saint. This means that the person is seen as **holy**. In the strict sense, a saint is someone who is in Heaven because of a holy life. **Canonized** saints are those whom the Church has officially declared as holy people worthy of imitation and **veneration**. Churches are named for them, and they are depicted in art with a **halo**. In a general sense, every member of the Church is a saint, redeemed by Jesus. This is what is meant by the **Communion of Saints**.

Salvation

Salvation is rescue from danger and evil. The greatest evil is **sin** because it leads to eternal death. Jesus saved us from sin by dying on the cross. His death atoned for all sin and made it possible for everyone to live forever with God again in perfect bliss.

Salvation History

Salvation History is the unfolding of God's plan to save humankind and bring us all to live with him forever. It spans all time from the beginning of our existence to the end of the world. The Bible contains the story of Salvation History, in particular God's dealings with his Chosen People, the life of the Savior, and the coming of the **Holy Spirit**. Salvation History continues in the life of the **Church**.

Samaria/Samaritan

Samaria was the province in the Holy Land between Israel and Judah. The Samaritans, originally Jews, intermarried with the Assyrians who conquered Israel in 622 BC The Samaritans developed their own version of Judaism and had their own temple. The Jews hated the Samaritans and avoided their territory. Jesus, however, made a Samaritan the hero in his parable the Good Samaritan. (Luke 10:25–37) Of the ten cured lepers, only the Samaritan returned to thank Jesus. (Luke 17:11–19) Then, too, Jesus met a Samaritan woman at a well and led her and her village to faith in him. (John 4:5–42)

sanctifying grace

Sanctifying grace is God's life within us, which makes us holy. It is permanent unless someone totally rejects God by committing a **mortal sin**. We first receive sanctifying grace at **Baptism** as a free gift from God.

sanctuary

A sanctuary is the part of the church around the altar where church rituals are centered. It is set off from the rest of the church by a railing, by being raised, or by its shape.

sanctuary lamp

When we walk into a church or chapel, we can always tell that the **Blessed Sacrament** is present if the sanctuary lamp is burning. This is a light fueled by wax or oil that is kept burning where the Blessed Sacrament is reserved. It is generally in a red glass container and suspended by a chain.

Sanhedrin

The Sanhedrin was the highest Jewish court at the time of Jesus. It had seventy-one members and met in the Temple area. The high priest, who was the spiritual leader and regarded as a king, probably presided over the Sanhedrin when Jesus was tried and condemned.

Satan
See **devil**.

Savior
See **Jesus**.

scapular
1) A scapular is part of a **habit** worn by some religious communities. It is a long, narrow cloth with a hole in the center for the head so that it can be worn to cover the front and back.

2) A scapular is a **sacramental** worn by **laypeople** who are invested in it by a priest. Wearing a scapular is a reminder to live a certain way of life and shows devotion to God or Mary. It is two small pieces of cloth joined by two cords. A scapular **medal** is another form. The Church has approved eighteen different scapulars, but the most popular is the brown scapular of Our Lady of Mount Carmel.

schism (SIZ-um or SKIZ-um)
A schism is the separation of a group from the **Roman Catholic Church**. In 1054, cultural and political differences led to the split between the Eastern (Greek) and Western (Latin) churches. The **Eastern Churches** are the Orthodox churches. The Great Western Schism refers to the Church turmoil that occurred during 1378 and 1417. Three different **popes** were elected, and national groups lined up behind each one.

scribes
During the time of Jesus, the scribes were experts in the law and took care of legal documents. Most of them were **Pharisees**, and in general they opposed Jesus.

Scripture
See **Bible.**

scruples
Scruples are unreasonable worries about a moral act and the state of one's soul. Someone with scruples is plagued with unnecessary guilt and may refrain from acting out of fear that something is wrong when it actually is not.

seal of confession
The seal of confession is the priest's obligation not to reveal anything told to him in the Sacrament of **Penance.** A priest who breaks this seal is excommunicated. Saint John Nepomucene is known for refusing to tell the king of Bohemia what his wife confessed. The king had John thrown in a river where he drowned and became known as the "martyr of the confessional."

Second Vatican Council
See **Vatican Council II.**

secular institute
A secular institute is an organization of **laypeople** and priests who are consecrated to God by private **vows** of poverty, chastity, and obedience. The members do not live in community. They attempt to sanctify the world through living and working within it.

seminarian
A seminarian is a man who is preparing for the priesthood. He lives and studies in a seminary where he is formed to administer the **sacraments** and minister to people. Seminarians study philosophy, and after graduating they study theology for four or five years.

seminary
See **seminarian.**

sermon
See **homily**.

Sermon on the Mount
The Sermon on the Mount is the discourse (long talk) of Jesus primarily found in Matthew 5:1—7:27. It includes the **Beatitudes**, the **Lord's Prayer**, moral laws, and a few **parables**. Luke's Gospel has a shorter version in which Jesus speaks on a plain (Luke 6:20–49). By having Jesus stating laws on a mount, Matthew likens him to **Moses**, who received the Ten **Commandments** on Mount Sinai.

shrine
A shrine is a sacred place for prayer dedicated to Jesus or a holy person. People make **pilgrimages** to shrines such as the National Shrine of St. John Neumann in Philadelphia, Pennsylvania. Churches may have shrines within them. Shrines may be set up in homes to show devotion to Jesus or a saint. For example, in May it is a custom to place a statue of Mary in a special place and decorate it with flowers. This Marian shrine is known as a May altar.

Sign of the Cross
The Sign of the Cross is the prayer accompanied by the gesture signifying that we follow Jesus who saved us through the cross. It combines our belief in the **Trinity** and in **redemption**. We make the Sign of the Cross at the beginning and end of our prayers. When entering and leaving a church, we make it with holy water and perhaps when we **genuflect**. **Blessings** are given by making the Sign of the Cross over someone or something. We also make the Sign of the Cross when we receive a blessing. You might see an athlete make the Sign of the Cross during competition.

To make the Sign of the Cross on ourselves, first we touch our forehead with our right hand and say, "In the name of the Father." Then we touch our lower chest and say, "and of the Son." Next we touch our left shoulder and say, "And of the Holy." We end by touching our right shoulder and saying, "Spirit. Amen." Among Hispanic Catholics, it is common to see people place their thumb across their forefinger to form a cross and kiss it after making the Sign of the Cross.

sin

Sin is freely and deliberately disobeying God. It shows a lack of love for God and sometimes for others and ourselves. Sin hurts our relationship with God and threatens our chance to live with him. The Israelites referred to sin as "missing the mark." This is apt because sin is a failure to be all that we were created to be. The consequence of the original, or first, sin was death. Jesus atoned for all sin and called everyone to repent.

A **mortal sin** is deadly. It is a serious sin that destroys grace, the life of God, in a person. Mortal sin makes it impossible to belong to God's kingdom. A **venial sin** is a lesser sin. All sins can be forgiven in the Sacrament of **Penance**. Social sin is the sinful situations and structures that exist in a society. It is the collective result of the sinful choices of individuals over time.

sister, religious

A sister is a woman **consecrated** to God who lives in community and follows the rule of a certain congregation. She makes **vows**, usually of poverty, chastity, and obedience, and wears a **habit** that identifies her as a member of her congregation. In popular speech, she is sometimes called a **nun**. A sister's life is devoted to prayer and service to the world in various **ministries**. Her home, where she usually lives with other sisters, is called a convent.

social justice

Social justice is the virtue of joining with others to promote the common good. It is based on the dignity of human beings created by God. Social justice entails promoting the rights of all people to a just wage;

freedom from oppression; fair treatment; freedom from discrimination; adequate food, shelter and clothing; and so on. Living the Gospel means working for social justice.

Son of Man

No one is sure what "Son of Man" means. The Book of Daniel in the Bible uses the term for someone who will come at the end of the world. It is also a title that Jesus used for himself, sometimes in connection with his suffering and his coming as judge at the end of the world. Son of Man refers to the humanity of Jesus, while Son of God refers to his divinity. The expression could simply be a way to refer to oneself, like "yours truly."

Sorrows of the Blessed Virgin Mary

The Sorrows, or Dolors, of the Blessed Virgin Mary is a devotion to the seven times that Mary experienced pain because she was the Mother of God. These sorrows are the prophecy of Simeon at the **Presentation**: the flight into Egypt, the loss of Jesus in the Temple, the way of the cross, the Crucifixion, the descent from the cross, and the burial of Jesus. Images of the Sorrowful Mother show her heart pierced with seven swords. We celebrate Our Lady of Sorrows on September 15, the day after the feast of the Triumph or Exaltation of the Cross. The seven joys of Mary is a parallel devotion.

soul

The soul is the spiritual, invisible part of a human being. The body is the material part. It is our soul that makes us in the image and likeness of God. Our soul has an intellect, which is the power to think, and a free will, which is the power to choose. Each soul is directly created by God and is immortal. At death the soul still lives, and at the end of the world, bodies and souls will be reunited.

spirit

A spirit has no matter and cannot be sensed. God is an uncreated spirit, and the **angels** are created spirits. We human beings have a material body and a spiritual soul.

Spiritual Works of Mercy

See **Works of Mercy.**

sponsors

See **godparents.**

Stations of the Cross

The Stations of the Cross, also called the Way of the Cross, is a devotion in memory of the suffering and death of Jesus. It began when people wanted to go on a **pilgrimage** to the **Holy Land** to walk the path Jesus took to **Calvary**, but they couldn't make the journey there. So instead they set up fourteen crosses in their own land, one for each event, and prayed in front of them. Later, images were added. Today the Stations of the Cross can be found inside all Catholic churches. Some religious places, such as **shrines** or retreat houses, may have Stations of the Cross outside.

We pray the Stations most often during **Lent.** It is the custom to genuflect before each station and pray, "We adore you, O Christ, and we praise you because by your holy Cross you have redeemed the world." Then we reflect on the suffering of Jesus depicted in the station. Some people add a fifteenth station, the **Resurrection.**

Here are the fourteen Stations of the Cross:

1. Jesus Is Condemned to Death
2. Jesus Carries His Cross
3. Jesus Falls the First Time
4. Jesus Meets His Mother
5. Simon of Cyrene Helps Jesus Carry His Cross

6. Veronica Wipes the Face of Jesus

7. Jesus Falls a Second Time

8. Jesus Consoles the Women of Jerusalem

9. Jesus Falls a Third Time

10. Jesus Is Stripped of His Garments

11. Jesus Is Nailed to the Cross

12. Jesus Dies on the Cross

13. Jesus Is Taken Down from the Cross

14. Jesus Is Laid in the Tomb

stigmata

The stigmata is the **supernatural** appearance of the wounds of the cru-cified Jesus in a person. The painful wounds occur in the hands and feet, the side, and the head. They may be invisible or visible, and if visible, they may bleed. Through the stigmata, a holy person shares in the sufferings of Jesus. The person who bears the wounds is a stigma-tist. Saint Francis of Assisi and, more recently, Saint Pio of Pietrelcina were stigmatists.

stipend

1) A stipend is money that a person freely offers to have a Mass said for an intention. When someone dies, friends and relatives may offer a stipend to have a Mass said for him or her.

2) A stipend is an amount given to anyone who performs a religious service, such as a talk at a parish.

stole

A stole is a long, narrow strip of material that is worn around the neck. Bishops and priests wear this vestment under the **chasuble** and hang-ing down the front. You can tell a **deacon** from a priest because a dea-con wears a stole over his left shoulder and across to the right side. Stoles are worn at Mass, during other sacraments, and when preaching.

Sunday
See **Sabbath**.

supernatural
Supernatural describes something that is beyond the power or nature of human beings. Being adopted as children of God is supernatural. **Grace** is supernatural.

surplice
A surplice is a loose, white, linen vestment with wide sleeves. It is about knee-length. A priest wears a surplice when administering a sacrament and in processions but not at Mass. It is worn over a cassock or a religious habit. Altar servers and **lectors** may also wear surplices.

Swiss Guards
The Swiss Guards are an army of one hundred men who are responsible for the pope's safety. They are Swiss Catholics between the ages of nineteen and thirty. Visitors to Rome like to have their picture taken with the Swiss Guards because of their colorful uniforms. Their ceremonial clothing is red, yellow, and blue and supposedly designed by Michelangelo. They wear a helmet with ostrich plumes. At other times they wear a blue uniform and a blue beret.

synod
1) A synod is a special meeting of **bishops** from different parts of the world that the pope calls to obtain their advice on an important Church issue. Recent synods have been on the Word of God, the Middle East, and the New **Evangelization**.
2) A meeting of a bishop and the clergy in his diocese is also called a synod.

Synoptic Gospels
The **Gospels** of Matthew, Mark, and Luke largely present the same events in the life of Jesus in the same order. For this reason, these

three Gospels are called the Synoptic Gospels. *Synoptic* means "viewed together." The Gospel of John is unique in many ways and is therefore not one of the Synoptic Gospels.

T

tabernacle

A tabernacle is the chest that houses the Blessed Sacrament in a church or chapel. It is locked because it holds the **ciborium** with consecrated hosts and a large host for exposition. The tabernacle is found in the **sanctuary** or in a side chapel. Look for the lighted sanctuary lamp, which is the sign that the Blessed Sacrament is present. During the **Exodus**, Moses had a tabernacle, or tent, built to house the **Ark** of the Covenant. The Israelites believed God was with them and spoke with them from above this chest.

temptation

We all experience temptations. Even Jesus was tempted by **Satan**. A temptation is something that entices us to sin. Some temptations come from the world, that is, what we see and hear and the influence of other people. Sometimes temptations come from the flesh, our own desires to do something wrong. And temptations may come from the devil, who can plant ideas for doing wrong in our mind. A temptation is not wrong, but giving in to it and sinning is wrong.

We find it hard to resist temptations because human beings became weak after the fall of **Adam** and **Eve**. However, with God's **grace** we can overcome these urges to turn against him. The more we pass the tests of temptations, the stronger we become. Doing good deeds, praying, and celebrating the Sacrament of **Penance** help us resist temptation.

testament

See **covenant**.

Theological Virtues

Theo is Greek for "God." The Theological Virtues are those that have to do directly with our relationship with God. They are faith, hope, and charity. These virtues are infused into us at **Baptism**. Faith is believing in God and his promises. Its symbol is the cross. Hope is relying on God to give us the grace to achieve Salvation. Its symbol is an anchor. And charity is loving God and loving others for his sake. Its symbol is a heart. In Heaven there will be no need for faith and hope. But love will last forever. Praying the Acts of Faith, Hope, and Love is a good way to grow in these virtues.

theology

Theology is the study of **God** and everything related to God. It investigates our beliefs with tools of reason assisted by **faith**. There are many fields of theology. They cover topics such as doctrines, Christ, the Church, the liturgy, and morality. The person who is trained in theology and works to understand and explain the Church's teachings better is called a theologian.

theophany (thee-AH-fuh-nee)

A theophany is a manifestation or showing of God. It could be an appearance or a direct communication. Examples are God speaking to Moses at the burning bush, the baptism of Jesus when the Trinity was present, and the Transfiguration, when Jesus appeared glorified.

theotokos (THEE-oh-TOH-kus)

Theotokos is the Greek word for "Mother of God." It is the Eastern Church's main title for **Mary**. This title was confirmed at the Council of Ephesus in 431. *Theotokos* is found in our oldest prayer to Mary, which begins, "We fly to thy patronage." This prayer is from about the year 250.

thurible

See **censer**.

tithe

To tithe is to donate a certain percentage of one's income to the Church. The Israelites tithed ten percent, and that is what some people give today. The money is used to support the Church and all its works. Church law obliges us to provide what is necessary to maintain the Church, the sacraments, and its ministers. We are asked to give our time, talent, and treasure to the Church that cares for our needs.

Torah

See **Pentateuch**.

Tradition

Tradition is the religious teachings and customs handed down orally or in writing. It is contained in our **creeds** and the documents of Church councils. **Scripture** and Tradition go hand in hand and contain all we need to know to be saved. Together they make up what is called the **Deposit of Faith**.

Transfiguration

The Transfiguration is the **theophany** when the glory of Jesus' divinity showed through his humanity in front of three of his **Apostles**. The **Synoptic Gospels** tell how Jesus took Peter, James, and John up to the top of a mountain. Jesus' face shone, and his clothes were bright white. **Moses** and the **prophet** Elijah appeared, and Jesus spoke with them about his coming suffering. The Apostles heard the voice of God call Jesus his beloved Son. Perhaps the purpose of the Transfiguration was to strengthen the faith of the Apostles in preparation for his Crucifixion. According to tradition, the Transfiguration took place on Mount Tabor. But some scholars claim that Mount Hermon is more likely.

transubstantiation

Transubstantiation is the change of bread and wine into the Body and Blood of Jesus. Although the substance of the bread and wine is changed, they look and taste the same. This change is brought about by the power of the Holy Spirit, the action of Jesus, and the words of the priest at the **Eucharist**.

triduum

A triduum is three days of prayer to prepare for a feast or a celebration or to ask for a certain grace or favor. Each year we observe the **Easter Triduum**.

Trinity

The Blessed Trinity is God the Father, God the Son, and God the Holy Spirit. They are Three Persons in one God. This is a basic mystery of our faith. The Three Persons are coequal (have the same powers) and coeternal (have no beginning and no end). The Son proceeds from the Father, and the Holy Spirit proceeds from the Father and the Son. They are bound together in love. Although the Persons in our Triune God act as one, we attribute a different work to each. We say that the Father is the Creator, the Son is the Redeemer, and the Holy Spirit is the Sanctifier.

Things in nature can help us understand the Trinity. Saint Patrick compared the Trinity to a three-leaf clover. The Trinity is also like the three forms of water (liquid, ice, vapor) or the three parts of an egg. In the end we will never completely understand the Trinity because it is a mystery.

U

Urbi et Orbi

Urbi et Orbi is Latin for "to the city [Rome] and to the world." It describes the **blessing** the pope gives from the balcony of St. Peter's

Basilica at Christmas and Easter. It comes after the pope speaks to the world and extends the season's greetings in many different languages. This papal blessing may also be given at a pope's inauguration and on special occasions.

V

Vatican Council II

The Vatican Council II, also referred to as the Second Vatican Council, held from 1962 to 1965, was the twenty-first ecumenical council. It was called by Pope John XXIII to renew and modernize the Church. The previous council, Vatican Council I, ended in 1870. About 2,500 bishops assembled at St. Peter's Basilica in Rome for Vatican Council II. This council produced sixteen documents on a variety of topics that served to guide the Church into the future. These documents are still studied and discussed today.

Vatican/Vatican City

The Vatican is the governing center of the Church located in Vatican City. It takes its name from Vatican Hill in Rome. The pope, who is the Bishop of Rome and the spiritual leader of the Church, resides there. The **Roman Curia** offices as well as St. Peter's Basilica, the Vatican Museums, and the Vatican Library are located at the Vatican. Vatican City, which is only 108.7 acres, is the smallest sovereign state in the world. About a thousand people live in Vatican City, and about four thousand people work there.

Venerable

See **canonization.**

veneration

1) Veneration is an act of reverence or deep respect. For example, on Good Friday we might venerate the cross by kissing it.

2) Veneration is honor and devotion given to the **saints**. It is called dulia and differs from the adoration given to God, which is called latria. The saints are worthy of our reverence and imitation because they lived holy lives. We ask the saints to pray for us just as we ask our friends on earth to pray for us.

venial sin

Venial sin is disobeying God's law in a way that does not completely remove grace, divine life, from us. However, venial sin does weaken our relationship with God. It is like an illness, not a death like **mortal sin**. An offense is venial when it is not a serious matter or when it was committed without sufficient knowledge, freedom, or full consent. Venial sins are forgiven when we are truly contrite and intend to avoid them in the future. They are forgiven by an Act of Contrition, prayers, good works, or receiving Holy Communion. But it is recommended that we confess venial sins in the Sacrament of **Penance**.

vestments

Vestments are the special garments that priests, deacons, and bishops wear for Mass and the sacraments. The color of the **chasuble** and **stole** matches the **liturgical color** of the season or feast being celebrated.

viaticum

Viaticum is the Eucharist given to a person who is dying. It is his or her last Communion. *Viaticum* is a Latin word that means "with you on the way." This Communion gives a person who is near the end of his or her life's journey the comfort of knowing that Jesus goes with him or her and gives him or her God's grace. Viaticum may be included in the Sacrament of the **Anointing of the Sick**. It is part of what used to be called the last sacraments or last rites.

Vicar of Christ

See **pope**.

vice

See **Capital sins**.

vigil

A vigil is the day or evening before a feast. Christmas, Easter, and Pentecost have special vigils. A vigil Mass on Saturday satisfies our Sunday obligation. We may also celebrate the Eucharist on the vigils of the **Holy Days of Obligation** instead of on the days themselves.

vigil light/votive light

In some churches and shrines, you see rows of candles in a rack. These are vigil lights, also called votive lights. People light them and say a prayer for a special intention or to honor God or a saint. The candle keeps vigil until it burns out. Ordinarily, people make a donation when lighting a vigil light. Some vigil lights are battery operated.

virtue

A virtue is a moral habit or power that enables us to perform good deeds. The word *virtue* is based on the Latin word for "man," which indicates that a virtue is a strength. Some virtues like the **Theological Virtues** are infused into us by God. Others are developed by repetition. The more we practice a virtue, the easier it becomes. With the help of the Holy Spirit and through our own efforts, our spiritual life grows, and we become holier. Virtues make us more like Jesus and keep us faithful to our covenant of love with God.

Visitation of Mary

The Visitation is the Blessed Virgin's stay with her older cousin Elizabeth in order to help her during her pregnancy. Mary made the journey while she herself was pregnant. At the sight of Mary, Elizabeth's baby, who was **John the Baptist**, leapt within her. On this occasion, Mary sang the Magnificat. In it she praised God for keeping the covenant made with Abraham by sending a Savior. The Visitation is the second Joyful Mystery of the Rosary.

See Luke 1:36–56 for the story of the Visitation.

vocation

1) A vocation is God's call to follow a certain way of life. All people have a vocation to holiness, to live in such a way that they are united with God.

2) Each person also has a call to a certain state of life. These vocations are the following: ordained, married, religious, and single. Knowing which state one is called to requires praying, talking to people, knowing oneself, and finding out more about each state.

votive Mass

A votive Mass is a Mass a priest can choose to offer on a day when no other solemnity, feast, or memorial Mass is assigned. Such a Mass has prayers for a special occasion or to honor some aspect of God or the saint. Some subjects of votive Masses are the Holy Trinity, the Sacred Heart, and the Blessed Virgin Mary.

vow

1) A vow is a solemn promise freely made to God to do good. It may be made publicly and received by a church representative, or it may be made privately. A vow may be temporary or permanent. Men and women religious usually vow to keep the **evangelical counsels** of poverty, chastity, and obedience. Our baptismal vows oblige us to reject Satan and serve God. We renew them at the Easter Vigil and on Easter.

2) A vow is a solemn promise made to another person. To fail to keep the promise is sinful. In the Sacrament of Matrimony, the partners make vows to each other.

W

Way of the Cross
See **Stations of the Cross**.

Word of God
1) The Word of God is a title for Jesus. He is known as the Word made flesh. He is also called the *Logos*, which is Greek for "Word." A word communicates. God communicates with us most fully through Jesus.
2) Sacred Scripture is the written Word of God in which he reveals himself to us.

Works of Mercy
The Works of Mercy are deeds of charity done out of compassion for people in need. The seven Corporal Works of Mercy are related to the body:

- Feeding the hungry
- Giving drink to the thirsty
- Clothing the naked
- Sheltering the homeless
- Visiting the sick
- Visiting the imprisoned
- Burying the dead

There are also seven Spiritual Works of Mercy:

- Admonishing the sinner
- Instructing the ignorant
- Advising the doubtful
- Comforting the afflicted
- Bearing wrongs patiently
- Forgiving injuries
- Praying for the living and the dead

worship
See **adoration**.

Y

Yahweh

Yahweh is the personal name of God that he revealed to Moses at the burning bush. The Hebrew language has no vowels, so originally this name was written as YHWH. Vowels were supplied later. The word *Jehovah* is a variation. The meaning of Yahweh is uncertain. Proposed interpretations include "I am who am," "I who create," and "I am here for you." Out of reverence for God, the Jews do not utter or write his name. They substitute *Adonai*, which means "the Lord." In Greek this is *Kyrie*, and in Latin it is *Dominus*. The word *Yahweh* is never used in the New Testament. Pope Benedict XVI decreed that it is not to be used in liturgy or in songs. This is because *Yahweh* is an unclear term, and refraining from using it shows sensitivity to our Jewish brothers and sisters.

Z

zucchetto (zoo-KET-o)

A zucchetto is a skullcap worn mostly by bishops. The pope's zucchetto is white, while other bishops wear a purple one. The zucchetto is worn under the **miter** and is removed during the Liturgy of the Eucharist.

About the Author

Mary Kathleen Glavich, SND, has developed faith formation material for more than 30 years. She has written over 70 books and worked on 5 textbook series, including *Christ Our Life*. She has taught every grade, and now blogs at www.kathleenglavich.org.

Also by Mary Kathleen Glavich, SND

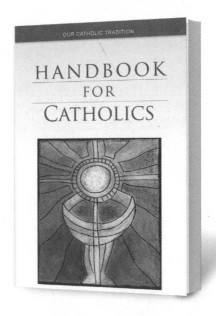

HANDBOOK FOR CATHOLICS
$3.50 • PB • 2855-1

Handbook for Catholics is a conveniently organized collection of all the essential information needed for lay Catholics to understand and practice the faith they profess. From common Catholic prayers to Catholic Doctrine, from the Liturgical Year Calendar to the Order of the Mass, this easy-to-read, easy-to-use book will help Catholics grow in their knowledge and love of the faith.